IN THIS MANNER, PRAY

DEVELOPING AN EFFECTIVE & FERVENT PRAYER LIFE

ERICA C. BETHELY

DEDICATION

This book is dedicated to my family, friends, and every person who has impacted my life, bible study group, and those I fellowship with. I am truly grateful to have each of you in my life. My life is amazingly blessed because of each of you. I am thankful to God for the rich deposits that each of you has made in my life. My prayer to both you and your families is that the Lord, the God of your ancestors, would increase and bless you a thousand times more, just as he promised to your forefathers. Blessed be our God who always causes us to triumph in victory. Be victorious in Jesus' name, amen.

Unlike the past, invaders will not take their houses,
and confiscate their vineyards.
For my people will live as long as trees,
and my chosen ones will have time to enjoy their hard-won gains.
They will not work in vain,
and their children will not be doomed to misfortune.
For they are people blessed by the LORD,
and their children, too, will be blessed.
I will answer them before they even call to me.
While they are still talking about their needs,
I will go ahead and answer their prayers!

Isaiah 65:22-24

CONTENTS

DEDICATION...4

PREFACE..8

INTRODUCTION..13

KEYS TO REMEMBER WHEN DEVELOPING A PRAYER LIFE....................16

JESUS TAUGHT HIS DISCIPLES HOW TO PRAY...................................21

SEEKING GOD..34

DEVELOPING YOUR PRAYER LIFE..41

PRAY IN THE NAME OF JESUS...63

YOU HAVE BEEN CHOSEN FOR THIS ASSIGNMENT............................72

SPIRITUAL WEAPONS FOR EFFECTIVE PRAYERS................................77

THE ARMOR OF GOD: DRESSING PROPERLY FOR PRAYER...................91

WHY DO WE KEEP PRAYING?...104

PRAYER WARRIORS OF THE BIBLE..117

SPECIFIC PRAYERS PETITIONS & SUPPLICATION 127

IN CLOSING...160

ABOUT THE AUTHOR...176

Prophetic Declarations Over Your Life

Death and life are in the power of the tongue, and those who love it will eat its fruit. You will speak life and not death and be abundantly blessed. God's Word supersedes every word that has been spoken over your life. Any weapon formed against your life or against your descendants will not prosper and is returned to the sender void. You shall be fruitful and multiply. You shall subdue and rule over the earth. You and your descendants shall know the voice of God and that of a stranger you will not follow. Your mind is covered under the blood of Jesus. Every word curse spoken over you or your descendants is broken by the power of the Holy Ghost. You shall walk in your God-given authority in the power of his strength. The joy of the Lord is your strength. The peace of God rest, rule, and abides in every area of your life and your family's life. When the enemies of your life and soul approach you or your family, or your household, the Lord will lift up a standard so strong that they will not be able to come against it. In Jesus' name, amen!

PREFACE

As I reflect upon my life and the developing phases of learning to pray, I can honestly say I had no idea of the true meaning and power of prayer. In the early stages of marriage, building a career and a family, God began to give me a strategy for how to pray over every area of my life. In the beginning, I worked for a company that was minutes away from my home. I would use my lunch break to come home and pray. During that time, I would read the Word of God and end in prayer. As I consistently did this, God began to reveal to me the hidden heart issues I was struggling with. I can remember spending time just weeping before the Lord.

While I was on my knees praying, I must confess that I was far from what and where I needed to be in life. I was filled with so much of what life dealt me, the choices I made, and the consequences thereof. Not fully understanding that God knew the plan he had for my life and that the plan was good, the plan would give me hope and a future to bring me to his expected end.

It took me years to understand who I was in Christ. Growing up, I was a victim of identity theft and labels. Yes, identity theft and labels. I didn't have the foggiest idea of who I was and why I even existed. Some labeled me as a tough, fearless kid, while others saw a girl who could be anything she wanted to be. The truth of the matter is that those who really knew me knew that I was the biggest cry baby in private. To this day, my mom says, "Here comes the weeping prophet." My siblings would say, "Don't mess with her. You know she has paper made feelings." As a child, we grew up in a home where we were devoted Catholics, went to Catholic school for a number of years, and later attended public school. Growing up Catholic, I admired the nuns and secretly swore in my heart that I would one day take the oath to become a nun. Boy, was I in for a rude awakening.

I can remember in my bible class, we had the task of learning the Ten Commandments and taking a test to see how well we had put them to memory. Let's just say it didn't go too well. I wrote them down as instructed and committed to learning them. When the test started, I took that paper out and sat on it to copy what I hadn't remembered. Ok, I cheated! Who hasn't? My teacher gave me the grace I didn't deserve. He never exposed that I was cheating. I later learned the power of healing from that same teacher. I came to school one day and wasn't feeling well. He asked me what was wrong, and I said my head hurts. He felt my head and said I appeared to have a fever. Instead of him sending me to the office to call for a ride home, he took his hands and placed them on my head and began to pray. By the time he finished praying, he asked, "How are you feeling?" I didn't want to answer him. The headache and the fever were gone, and I was staying at school. I remember him saying, you should be feeling better now.

As I approached adulthood, I no longer attended the Catholic Church, joined a different denomination, and accepted Jesus Christ as my Lord and savior. Later, I was baptized, and from there, I learned to read the Bible, attended Sunday school, fellowshipped, and began to develop impacting relationships. I purchased a bible and read a chapter a day. I learned to do this from a lady who managed the office I worked in while in high school. One day in her office, I mentioned to her that I started reading the Bible and her response was, "The more you read the Word of God, he takes what's not of Him out of you and puts what's of him inside of you. To this day, I remember that the Word cleanses you. I attended that church until I moved out of state.

Once I moved to Georgia, I experienced Christ in a new way. One of my coworkers invited me to church with her, and my life transformed in ways I never imagined. The praise and worship were awesome, and most Sundays, I believed that the pastor was speaking directly to me as if I was the only person in the congregation. This defining moment led me to make a different commitment to God and a denial of self. I approached reading the Word of God differently and wanted to know God's voice. I wanted to know that God was really real, and I wanted to experience his touch.

As an adult, I took a class that addressed your identity. The couple that taught the class gave us two books titled "Identity in Christ" and how to have "Victory Over Darkness." Both books were by an author by the name of Neil T. Anderson. These were the books the facilitators used to instruct the class along with the Word of God. After taking this class, I took on the identity of Christ and who I was in him. The Word says that if any man be in Christ, he is a new creature. There were times when this new identity would be tested. I daily made confessions of what I was learning, eagerly applying them to my life.

As I confessed these scriptures, I would look in the mirror at my face so that I would be reaffirmed of who I was. Also, I make it a point to say I am the righteousness of God in Christ Jesus; I am the salt of the earth; in Christ, old things are passed away, etc. Would you believe one day someone made a condescending remark implying that I was a nothing? "After all, you're a nobody," is what was said. As I stood there, listening to those words, my heart melted as the water began to form in my eyes. I looked them square in the eye and said, "I am the righteousness of God!" and walked away. As I prepared for class that night, I could not get past what was said. As I shared what happened in class, the leaders began to pray for me. A short time later, this person asked for forgiveness after having a heart-to-heart meeting that they requested. Later we established a very good working relationship, and they began to share with me issues they were facing and would request that I pray for them. Understand that the enemy of your soul does not want you to know who you are nor the power you have been given. He especially does not want you to walk in your God-given authority. I have witnessed the extremes of those who later thought I thought more of myself than I should. Always remember that who you are in Christ and what God has said about you is the only thing that matters. His Word defines who you are. There will be times when You will be tested in every area of your life, but God will grace you to get through it.

I pray that this book will give every reader a foundation in prayer on which they can build upon. I pray that you will apply these basic principles to your everyday life and walk in the freedom to be the intercessor God has called you to be. Now more than ever, we need to take our God-given authority and pray. Pray with such a vengeance until Hell is shaken by your very presence and that Satan is afraid of the damage that is being done to his kingdom through your prayer life. At the end of my life, I want it to be said that I was a Chosen Intercessor who chose to pray by choice and not by circumstance. This book was not designed to read in a short period of time but to equip every reader with tools that would impact their lives. Do not attempt to read this book in its entirety without putting in the time and the work needed to develop your gift.

Let's get started!

INTRODUCTION

This book was created for training and developmental purposes. I have spent many years studying books and the Word of God only to learn that it is the Lord who teaches us to pray. This study guide would not have been birthed without the leading of the Holy Spirit. At this point, I can honestly say life without prayer is unimaginable. It can be compared to a river with no water. Both equate to the same, "being dry and having no purpose."

As a child, being called to be an Intercessor was not known unto me. The first memory I have was after the death of my Father, my grandmother made all of the grandchildren stand/kneel in a line beside the bed, and she would lead us in prayer and teach us to repeat what she said. Our grandmother instructed us to kneel around the bed and pray to God. She always ended each prayer by asking God to bless my mom, dad, sisters, brothers, etc. She taught us to pray for others everywhere. As a child, I recalled thinking exactly how many people can God truly bless? My second memory of prayer and the funniest memory of prayer occurred nightly as my mom attempted to teach us "The Lord's Prayer" (Matthew 6:12). My mom would start by saying, "Our Father who art in heaven, hallowed be thy name, thy kingdom come, thy will be done...", but somehow we never got past "give us this day our daily bread." Every time we got to that point in the prayer, my baby sister would say, "I am hungry, may I have a piece of bread, mommy?" Off to the kitchen, she would go. Those moments will never be forgotten. I never understood why my mom would not bring the bread to prayer or just let her eat the bread before prayer. Who would have known this was the beginning of the purpose and plan God had for my life? Thirdly, I remember as a child, my mother would often pray in the car as we traveled out of town for protection, a safe trip, and safely returning home. Each of these defining moments established the foundation that I have passed on to my children. On several occasions, I heard my mom praying and asking God just to let her live to see her children grow up. God was more than faithful to her. My mom is a great grandmother as I write this book. Lastly, I remember my great aunt, who would sit in a corner with her Bible in her hand, reading and praying. Whenever I visited her home, she would be in her chair, in a corner doing the same thing as she took time to look over her glasses to acknowledge you were in the room.

Praying as a family can be difficult and hard at times, but it is needed. There have been times when I have directed some of my children to leave the prayer room because of the disturbance they created. Eventually, they understood that we have to be on the same page when it comes to prayer. I can remember the older siblings telling some of, the younger ones, please don't act up this will only make us have to be here longer. Often, I reminded them that I have a prayer life, and they must understand the need for a personal prayer life for themselves. When they are grown and on their own, they will have to go to God for themselves. As parents, we must make every effort to teach them how to go to

God on their own behalf. They will have to know how to seek him, get in his Word, and pray. As parents, we will never stop praying for our children; however, certain situations and events will occur in their lives that only they and God can work out together.

As you navigate the book, you will find a list of keys to help develop your prayer life. While studying this material, you are encouraged to use your Bible, a dictionary, thesaurus, a highlighter, notebook, and a pen. This will help further your studying on prayer and create a more personal, intimate relationship with you and God. Remember, this is just a starting place because it is the Lord who *teaches us to pray*.

CHAPTER ONE
KEYS TO REMEMBER WHEN DEVELOPING A PRAYER LIFE

As we begin this chapter, the goal is to set a foundation on the basic principles of prayer, define what prayer is, and identify how to effectively demonstrate the power of prayer in each reader's life. Consider what makes prayer truly effective in the lives of individuals. Before you start reading this book, I respectfully request that you set aside time for yourself daily to get the rest that you need to constantly spend time with God. This adjustment can be hard, but it will be worth it.

Let us discuss what prayer is. Prayer is simply communication with God, having a conversation with God. Many of us believe that communication is a one-sided street. In other words, we do all the talking and never take time to truly listen for a response. Many of my friends will tell you that I will take over a conversation and when I am finished, I will say love you and talk to you later. When, in fact, effective communication is talking, listening, and responding appropriately. Many of us rush into prayer with our own agenda. We have our prayer list of needs, wants, and desires and never speak to God before we even make a request. One of the first things I do when I arise is say good morning Father, good morning Holy Spirit and good morning Jesus, and then I proceed with I love you and thank you for this day. Lord, please let me be an effective witness for your kingdom today. I desire to represent God in a way that is pleasing to him. I never care about myself. I only care about my representation of him and him alone. We can all agree that this may sound strange. However, there have been times when I must confess that I did not always see it this way. This was something that I had to learn and still face all the time. I have concluded that there are certain people in life who God will use to grow you in certain areas of your life that will rub you the wrong way. The agitation is sometimes necessary. It is so important to put on the whole armor of God. We will discuss this in a later chapter.

The most effective prayer is to pray the will of God. To pray the will of God is to pray the Word of God by incorporating God's promises in the scriptures in your prayers and always praying in the name of Jesus! There are many examples in both the Old and New Testament of individuals who fervently prayed. One of the best prayer models we can emulate is that of Jesus Christ. You may admire or desire to pray like someone you know. Understand that what you hear is their communication (their prayer language) with the Father that has developed over time. To be an effective prayer leader or have an effective prayer ministry, one must have a very strong prayer life. I remember a woman whose prayer life I admired. I admired her prayer life so much that I would go home after service and try to pray just as she did, only to find out I was getting nowhere. After getting to know her and one of her sisters on a more personal level, I learned that their mother was a woman of prayer, and her family once faced many difficulties in their lives, which led them to seek God in prayer. This not only developed her prayer life but established the fearless person she became. To this day, I can remember going on movie dates with both of them, and we developed a bond of sisterhood. I had the privilege of being taught by them in some bible study classes. One night while I was sitting in one of their classes, one of them stressed the importance of knowing who we were in Christ and the freedom that comes with it. She had each person in the class to confess their fears, what they had been told or believed about themselves. Once we did this, we had to renounce it. We were challenged to think differently. Until we learn who we are in Christ, and it is in him who our identity is defined, we will continue to be defeated. Christ died for us to live a victorious life.

I had the privilege to hear the testimonies of one of their husbands, the illness he faced, and the financial difficulties that came with it. I asked God to forgive me for attempting to be like someone else in prayer. The message here is, to be like someone else who has an anointed prayer life, you must be willing to endure his or her hardships, trial struggles, etc. I learned that the only way I could ever pray like her was to go through what she went through. To whom much is given, much is required. Therefore, the Holy Spirit taught me to pray as I studied God's Word and as I spent time with God. While studying the Word of God, I would read aloud and write out scriptures to commit them to memory. As I read chapters that addressed sin (missing God's mark or standard), I would repent of my sins and ask God to forgive me and the generations that preceded my generation. I would also ask God to reveal sins committed by my husband's and my bloodline in my quiet time. I would renounce them and ask God to let them stop with our generation. I would also ask him to remove them. Clearly understand that the sins of the Father will visit the children of the disobedient. As I matured in life, a dear friend shared with me that some things are not just generational curses. They're learned behaviors developed over time. It is so important to be as honest as possible with your children. The truth can hurt, but it will make you free.

When I read scriptures that covered blessings, I would declare those blessings over my life, claiming them over my household, loved ones, friends, church, schools, nation, and our government. One year, our economy turned for the worst. Some people lost their homes, investment accounts plunged, and careers took a different path that no one was prepared for. It appeared as if life had taken a trip down uncertainty street. I remember going into my prayer closet and falling on my knees with tears streaming down my face. I could not understand what was going on. Once I finished talking to the Lord, he said to me that this wasn't about me. God revealed to me his heart and what needed to happen. When I left my prayer closet, I never questioned what was going on again.

I called a dear friend of mine, and I said not one of my friends, family, or any of their friend's families was going to participate in this recession. I gave her the scripture that we would stand on, and we confessed it daily. We post this scripture in certain areas of our homes to ensure the Word stays in our paths. My dear friend began to call her family and friends and decreed the same thing over them. We prayed Psalm 115:14. The Lord shall increase you more and more, you and your children. One year she gave a money pouch with this scripture and a penny inside. Sounds like an increase to me.

As you grow in prayer, you will learn that prayer is more precise than considering God your personal vending machine or ATM. Prayer is not defined by time or length. Prayer should consist of seeking, asking, knocking, listening, and waiting for an answer. I am in a place in my life where I just turn on praise and worship music, light a candle while I sing, grab one of my prayer garments, and dance before the Lord. It amazes me that while I am worshiping the King of Kings, the Lord of Lords, He shows me His love, His grace, His presence, daily prayer assignments, and His plans for my life, family, and others.

CHAPTER KEYS

1. Identify sin.
2. Sincerely ask for forgiveness.
3. Repent.
4. Be Consistent.

CHAPTER TWO
JESUS TAUGHT HIS DISCIPLES HOW TO PRAY

When I was a stay-at-home mom, I desired to know more about God, who he is, his nature. I attended a Women's conference where a prophet there really made an impression on my life. I went to the resource table, and he had a book called The Names of God. I instantly purchased that book, grabbed a highlighter and a notepad, and began to dig in. What a revelation. This is relevant because, in many scriptures, Jesus often referred to his Father. He made it very clear that the Father was in charge. Therefore, it is important if we expect to receive anything from the Father, then we must know how to approach him and what to call him when we approach him. Let us take a moment here to read Matthew 6:5-14. Once you read this scripture, review the scriptures on God's names, his attributes, and apply them to the model prayer at the end of the chapter. While conducting a search on my own, I stumbled on a site called GotQuestoin.com that I used to further my study. I added the names of God from this site to this chapter to assist you in learning the names of God and the different attributes of God. Be sure to look them up according to the coordinating scriptures, write them out and commit them to memory.

I recommend taking a few at a time. This is not about gathering information. It is about getting to know who God is according to his Word and applying this wisdom to your life. Scripture tells us to hide God's Word in our hearts so that we will not sin against him. Knowing the very nature of God, who he is, and what he does will put things in proper perspective and help you properly approach him to get what you need in prayer. Growing up, I never had a father, so it was hard for me to identify what a father really was or meant. Now that I have children, I have begun to understand the natural side of having a father in your life. There have been times when I have asked my children to do something, and they will respond with, but my daddy said. We all know that when you use the word "but," everything in front of it is canceled out. In other words, just disregard what you have said because this is what is going to happen. When you know who your Father is and what he says, nothing else matters. His words have authority, and his name carries weight and power!

Jesus taught His disciples to pray by giving them instructions found in Matthew 6:5-14. His instructions gave the disciples a foundation of how they should and should not pray. Upon studying the specifics of this text, this is the template Jesus taught His disciples to pray.

Matt. 6:9 *Our Father who art in heaven, may your **name** be kept holy.* Here is where we take a moment to reflect on and pray the names of God.

THE NAMES OF GOD

ADONAI
Genesis 15:2
Judges 6:15

EL, ELOAH
Nehemiah 9:17
Psalm 139:19
Genesis 31:29
Numbers 23:19
Deuteronomy 5:9-10
Nehemiah 9:31

ELOHIM
Genesis 17:7
Jeremiah 31:33
Genesis 1:1

EL ELYON
Deuteronomy 26:19

EL-GIBHOR
Isaiah 9:6
Revelation 19:15

EL-OLAM
Psalm 90:1-3

EL ROI
Genesis 16:1-14

EL SHADDAI
Genesis 49:24
Psalm 132:2,5

YAHWEH-ELOHIM
Genesis 2:4
Psalm 59:5

YAHWEH / JEHOVAH
Deuteronomy 6:4
Daniel 9:14
Exodus 3:14
Psalm 107:13
Psalm 25:11
Psalm 31:3

YAHWEH-JIREH
Genesis 22:14

YAHWEH-M'KADDESH
Leviticus 20:8
Ezekiel 37:28

YAHWEH-NISSI
Exodus 17:15

YAHWEH-RAPHA:
Exodus 15:26

YAHWEH-ROHI:
Psalm 23:1

YAHWEH-SABAOTH
Isaiah 1:24
Psalm 46:7

YAHWEH-SHALOM
Judges 6:24

YAHWEH-SHAMMAH
Ezekiel 48:35
Ezekiel 8—11
Ezekiel 44:1-4

YAHWEH-TSIDKENU:
Jeremiah 33:16
2 Corinthians 5:21

Matt. 6:10 *May your Kingdom come soon. May your will be done on earth, as it is in heaven.* God desires that his divine will be done in the earth through us as we operate in our God-given heavenly authority.

Matt. 6:11 *Give us today the food we need.* Tell God what you need from him spiritually, emotionally, and physically. God is Jehovah Jireh, our provider. He is also our healer, redeemer, comforter, etc.

Matt. 6:12 *and forgive us our sins, as we have forgiven those who sin against us.* If we confess our sins, he will forgive us. Confessing your sins will keep the enemy from having an accusation against you in the presence of God. It does not mean he will not try. It just will not work. There is freedom and peace that comes from forgiving yourself and others. Do some deep soul searching about this. I had to forgive God for not having a Dad. I was in my late twenties when God revealed this to me. I also had to forgive myself for all of the wrong choices I made. Sometimes, we have sinned against ourselves without any knowledge of it. I will admit that I have carried offenses against people for years only to discover that people move on with their lives. Some of them never knew they offended me. They were on their assignment, God sent or not. Remember what they mean for bad or evil God will work it out for your good.

Matt. 6:13 *and do not let us yield to temptation but rescue us from the evil one.* What is temptation? God's Word teaches us that God will provide us a way of escape when we are tempted. Confess your temptations and trials. Trust me, God already knows. Be free in Jesus' name. When the enemy comes back with it as a reminder, just do what I do. God, I thank you that you have already forgiven me of that and will continue to provide me a way of escape to stand in victory over it. Now prove your Word.

Matt. 6:14 *If you forgive those who sin against you, your heavenly Father will forgive you.* No explanation is needed. Now that you have studied how Jesus taught His disciples to pray, reflect on what you have learned. Write down any scriptures that grasp your heart in this next section. It is ok if none of them stand out to you at this very moment. Learning to meditate and apply the Word of God in prayer is your greatest weapon, both offensively and defensively against the enemy.

If you have ever been in a corporate or private setting during prayer, you will notice that people pray in different postures. Some people stand while praying. Others walk, kneel, bow, stand, or lay prostrate.

This occurs for a different reason. As you age, you may not be able to stand for long periods of time, resulting in just sitting in a chair or using a bench. Some kneel just out of reverence to God. I have a prayer pillow that I kneel or sit on depending on what I am led to do while praying. I fractured my left leg one afternoon after marching to the band hall in the rain after a football game. One of the band members ran into me by accident and caused me to fall. I have to wear a splint on and off for short periods in my life. As a result, I now slightly limp when I walk. I also have a bench and a recliner where I just sit sometimes while I pray, meditate, or talk to the Lord. There was an elderly person at the church I attend who would climb up and down the staircase during prayer and never missed a beat. This person could cover the entire Sanctuary without slowing down. I probably would have collapsed midway!

POSTURES IN PRAYER

Let us take a moment to discuss different types of prayer postures. These can be incorporated into your day-to-day prayer journey. Please review and search other scriptures to support praying postures, not limiting yourselves to what is being discussed in the sections. As you grow in this area, God will direct you. They are not in any particular order. Once you study them, see how you can implement them into your prayer life. Please be led by the Spirit of God during your prayer time. Getting in his presence and making reverence to God is what matters most.

BOWING: According to Webster's dictionary, the word bowing means bend the head or upper part of the body as a sign of respect, greeting, or shame. Express (thanks,

BOWING

agreement, or other sentiments) by bending one's head respectfully, bend the body to see or concentrate, bend with age or under pressure, submit to pressure or to someone's demands

- **Psalm 95:6** (NLT) Come, let us worship and bow down. Let us kneel before the Lord, our maker.

- **Exodus 34:8** (NLT) Moses immediately threw himself to the ground and worshiped.

- **Nehemiah 8:6** (NTL) Then Ezra praised the LORD, the great God, and all the people chanted, "Amen! Amen!" as they lifted their hands. Then they bowed down and worshiped the LORD with their faces to the ground.

- **Psalm 72:11** (NASB) May all kings bow before him; all nations serve him.

KNEELING: Merriam-Webster dictionary states that kneeling is to position the body so that one or both knees rest on the floor. It is a sign of lowering oneself or humbling oneself to God.

KNEELING

- **1Kings 8:54** (NASB) After Solomon finished offering this entire prayer and petition to the LORD, he rose from before the altar of the LORD, where he had been kneeling, hands outstretched toward heaven.

- **Luke 22:41-42** (NASB) Jesus is praying to God and does the following: 41 After withdrawing about a stone's throw from them and kneeling, he prayed, 42saying, "Father, if you are willing, take this cup away from me; still, not my will but yours be done."

- **1King 18:42** (NASB) So Ahab went up to eat and drink. But Elijah went up to the top of Carmel; and he crouched down on the earth and put his face between his knees.

- **Ezra 9:5** (NLT) At the time of the sacrifice, I stood up from where I had sat in mourning with my clothes torn. I fell to my knees and lifted my hands to the LORD my God.

STANDING

Standing: not moveable or a position from which one may assert or enforce legal rights and duties (Merriam-Webster Dictionary). One may use the standing position in prayer to indicate authority doing warfare prayers or stands up to make decrements and declarations unto the Lord.

- **Exodus 3:5** (NLT) Do not come any closer, the LORD warned. Take off your sandals, for you are standing on holy ground.

- **Exodus 33: 10** (NLT) When the people saw the cloud standing at the entrance of the tent, they would stand and bow down in front of their own tents.

Lay Prostrate: Stretched out with face on the ground in adoration or submission. This position is a symbol of trust and vulnerability.

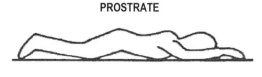

PROSTRATE

Here is where you are completely humbled and yielded in the presence of God.

- **Deuteronomy 9:25** (NIV) I lay prostrate before the LORD those forty days and forty nights because the LORD had said he would destroy you.

Walking: to advance or travel on foot at a moderate speed or pace; proceed by steps; move by advancing the feet alternately so that there is always one foot on the ground in bipedal locomotion and two or more feet on the ground in quadrupedal locomotion. In prayer, this indicates taking back territory or taking authority over the atmosphere where your feet are treading.

WALKING

- **2 Kings 4:35** Elisha got up, walked back and forth across the room once, and then stretched himself out again on the child. This time the boy sneezed seven times and opened his eyes!

Hands Raised: to elevate one hand up in the air. People normally hold their hand in the air during prayer or worship as a sign of surrender or in awe. Lifting one's hands could also be considered coming into agreement and alignment with the Word, the will, and the spirit of God, knowing that anything that we ask in the name of Jesus will be done.

HANDS RAISED

- **Leviticus 9:22** After that, Aaron raised his hands toward the people and blessed them. Then, after presenting the sin offering, the burnt offering, and the peace offering, he stepped down from the altar.

- **1 King 8:54** When Solomon finished making these prayers and petitions to the LORD, he stood up in front of the altar of the LORD, where he had been kneeling with his hands raised toward heaven.

- **Daniel 12:7** The man dressed in linen, who was standing above the river, raised both his hands toward heaven and took a solemn oath by the One who lives forever, saying, "It will go on for a time, times, and half a time. When the shattering of the holy people has finally come to an end, all these things will have happened."

- **1 Timothy 2:8** In every place worship, I want men to pray with holy hand lifted up to God, free from anger and controversy.

Prayer Demonstration

Our Father, who art in heaven hallowed be thy holy name. Lord, your name is Jehovah, meaning you are God. You are God and God alone. There is no other God besides you and by whom we call upon, who hears us and who answers us. Your name is Jehovah Jireh, and you are my (our) provider. Thank you for providing everything I (we) need in the name of Jesus. You are Jehovah Nissi, the Lord of our banner and righteousness, you are my (our) battle-ax and rear guard, you are the keeper of my (our) soul(s), you are the great all sufficient all-knowing God. You are the Alpha and the Omega, my (our) beginning and my ending. In you, I (we) move, breathe, and have my (our) being. I (we) exist because of you and you alone. You are Jehovah Rapha, the Lord who heals me (us) in every area of my (our) lives. Thank you for your healing power. Heal (my) our mind(s), bodies, spirits, and souls in the name of Jesus. Lord, we need you to heal us emotionally, physically healing, mentally, and spiritually in the name of Jesus. Lord, I (we) acknowledge that I (we) need you, and apart from you, I (we) cannot do anything but fail.

Your kingdom come, you will be done in the earth as it is in heaven, be done in our lives, your kingdom come in our homes. Your kingdom come in our president, senators, legislators, and our congressional representatives. Your kingdom come in all branches of government (legislative, executive, and judicial). Your kingdom come in our law enforcement agencies (state troopers, highway patrol officers, police officers, sheriffs, deputy sheriffs, etc.). Your kingdom come in our military (Army, Air Force, Navy, Marine, Coast Guard).

Your kingdom come in our school system (superintendent, assistant superintendent, deans, administrators, academic advisors, counselors, teachers, bus drivers, athletic directors, band instructors, orchestra conductors, cheerleading coaches, dance instructor, resource officers, secretaries, dietitians, custodians, etc.). Your kingdom come in our churches, our leadership, every Bishop, Pastor, Worship Leader, Teacher of the Word, Discipleship (cell or life) Group leaders. Your kingdom come in their homes, in their families and communities. Your kingdom come in our business, careers, and communities. Give us this day our daily bread. Lord, your Word says that you already know what we need before we ask. Your Word also says that we should make our request known unto you and that we have the petitions we have asked. Therefore, we are asking you to provide what we need. Lord, I (we) have need of_____. Forgive us of our trespass as we forgive those who have trespass or is indebted to us. Lord, I forgive myself for_____. I also forgive and release _____ for. Now that I have forgiven them Lord I ask that you would forgive me for _____. Lord, please bring to my remembrance anyone whom I have offended or who has offended me so that my prayers will not be hindered or my process blocked. I release everyone who has hurt me knowingly or unknowingly. I release everyone who has offended me, set up pits for my family or me. I walk in forgiveness, even when it hurts. Lord, I pray that every person I have offended, hurt, or misjudged would forgive me and release me from the offense. In Jesus' name. Lead us not into temptation but deliver us from the evil one. Lord, I know that Satan is the accuser of the brethren, and whatever his plan is for my life will not work because I am forgiven. Lord, your Word says that no temptation has overtaken you but that which is common to man, but when I (we are) am tempted Lord, you are faithful to provide us a way of escape that we will be able to stand under it. Lord, whatever is in me or my family, reveal it to us so that we will not be tempted or fulfill those desires. I release my family and myself from the sins of our past and from our bloodline, In Jesus' name, amen.

Please note that the Lord will give you a clear direction on how and when to pray. This is simply a means to get you started. Keep building your foundation in prayer.

 CHAPTER KEYS

1. Praying the names of God gives us access to the specific request that we make.
2. Understanding the pattern that Jesus gave us on approaching God is important for us to get into his presence and receive what we're requesting.
3. There are ways to approach God. The most important thing we have to remember, regardless of the posture that you pray in, we must be humble,

we must be honest and transparent, and we must believe that God can and will do what we are requesting, even if his answer is not what we were expecting. We understand that God is sovereign. However, he chooses whether or not to answer our request and does what is best for us.

Prophetic Declarations Over Your Life

Your children shall walk in the ways of God, and his covenant will be established with them. The Lord will cause a remnant in your family to serve him and draw others to his kingdom. The Lord will draw you and your family with love and kindness. The Lord will make his face to shine upon you and give you perfect peace that comes from him and him alone. Everything you experience in life will work out for your good and draw you closer to him, the only true and living God. You shall see miracles, signs, and wonders in your generation. God has chosen you to do a good work, and he will finish the good work he has started in you until the return of Christ Jesus, our Lord. In Jesus' name. Amen!

CHAPTER THREE
SEEKING GOD

Seek the kingdom of God above all else, and live righteously,
and he will give you everything you need. **Matthew 6:33**

The Word *kingdom*, as defined by the student bible dictionary, "refers to a king's authority or rule over a territory or over the hearts of people as in the kingdom of God." When we seek God, we are in search of his presence (his face). We surrender our will to his. It becomes our priority. Seeking God requires that we do it with our whole heart, mind, body, spirit, and soul. If you were asked how to seek God, how would you answer this? Refer to the scripture above.

According to the Tyndale Holy Bible dictionary, *seeking* means to go in search of, to ask for, and to try to acquire or gain. Seek God consistently by spending time with Him in prayer. Meditate on His Word daily. This will allow God to develop every area of your life by strengthening you both mentally and spiritually. When you see people who have a strong prayer life, many things have occurred. They have spent a great deal of time with God. They have studied the scriptures, sought God for deliverance, healing, and victory over every circumstance. Others were raised in a home where prayer was foundational, accompanied by an enhanced fervent desire to sustain a life of God's perfect will.

REFLECTION: Before you move on, take some time today and seek God's voice. Seek his direction. Seek his will for your life and your next steps. Knowing that God wants us to *know* his voice lets us know that there are other voices that do not come from him. It is not his desire that we follow strange voices.

I have found that God answers prayers that one prays based on His will. We have to seek Him to discern what His will is. Be confident in knowing that God will answer your prayers. Scripture teaches us that God will not turn away our prayers. We must comply within the confines of the will of God. Sin is what takes us out of the will of God. Most people have categories for sin, but to God, sin is just plain old sin. There is no big sin or little sin. God defines sin as not being obedient. When you know what is considered right/wrong and choose to do otherwise, it is sin. Envy, jealousy, strife, lust, anger, attitudes, lack of faith, gossip, murder, pride, gluttony, greed, selfishness, arrogance, resentment, folly, speaking evil over people, rejoicing over the failure or fall of another person, and the list goes on. All of which we have been guilty of at one time or another. The Word of God says that if we say we have not sinned, we are a liar, and the truth is not in us. Sin is not keeping our God-given assignment, not honoring your Word. It separates us from God and hinders our prayers. The Bible teaches us that God doesn't hear the prayers of sinners except they are prayers of repentance.

In your quiet time, ask God to reveal to you the hidden things in your heart. His Word says that we should hide his Word in our hearts so that we do not sin against him. On numerous occasions, I have gone to God and asked him to reveal to me the secrets of my heart, unconfessed sin, things I despise, and to reveal the sins that are in my bloodline. Over a period, God began to reveal them. Some of which I was not ready to confront, and some of which I am guilty of being a repeated offender. Sins of the flesh will kill you. I am going to be transparent here. One of my biggest challenges I ever faced was anger, followed by unforgiveness. For a very long time, I would give people a pass on what they did, while over time, I couldn't shake what they continually did. These two are in a constant battle with each other. Anger and unforgiveness are partners, in my opinion. Not properly addressed, they will lead you on a path that could be hard to rebound from. Facing people who have disappointed you, can leave you in a place of distrust. The life of an intercessor can be challenging. You are often pulled between your desire to please God and pray for others while simultaneously dealing with your own issues. The assignment of intercession is not for perfect people. It's for obedient, submitted people of faith.

FURTHER STUDY

- 2 Chronicles 15:1-4
- 2 Chronicles 7:14-15
- Hebrews 11:6
- Matthew 12:31
- Matthew 7:7-8
- Proverbs 3:6

EXERCISE

Let us use this section to put what we've read into action. Use the space provided to make a list of the things you know you need to get rid of. Even if you are not comfortable with writing them in this book. Take a separate sheet of paper and write them out. Let us go a step further. We are going to confess the sin so that God will forgive us, recite the prayer, then take a match, and burn the list as a symbol of them no longer having power over you. Do not be surprised if God has you to write a note to someone or make a phone call. Be prepared in the event they respond negatively. It's ok. They have a right to feel how they wish. God will deal with the matter.

_____

_____

_____

_____

_____

_____

_____

PRAYER

Lord, I repent of all of my sins. Please forgive me for every time I have _____. I confess that I have sinned against you and man. Please restore love where I have been disappointed and bring the healing that I need. Help me to overcome all of what life has offered me. Please forgive me for not walking in forgiveness towards _____. I acknowledge that what was done hurt me and caused me to be disappointed. Please restore trust where it was broken. I release all of those who have hurt me, and I release myself from the Spirit of offense. I walk in love even when I hurt. In Jesus' name. Amen

APPLICATION

Elijah prayed that it would not rain, and God did not allow rain to fall upon the earth for three years and six months. How do we know that he prayed the will of God? 1King 17-18:41;19:8 addressed this. In one chapter, God says it was not going to rain. Then Elijah prays for the rain to stop, and it did because God had already spoken it. In the very next chapter, God said it would one day rain again. Elisha prays for rain, and the Lord allowed the rain to come, and the earth brought forth its fruit again. James 5:17-18 reinforces this. Elijah was as human as we are, and yet when he prayed earnestly that no rain would fall, none fell for three and a half years! Then, when he prayed again, the sky sent down rain, and the earth began to yield its crops.

Study the following supporting scriptures showing how God hears and answers our prayers.

- **Psalm 66:19-20**
  But certainly, God has **heard**; He has given heed to the voice of my prayer. Blessed be God, Who has not turned away my prayer or His loving-kindness from me.

- **Philippians 4:6**
  Be anxious for nothing, but in everything by prayer and supplication, with thanksgiving, let your request be **made known** to God.

- **Isaiah 55:6-7**
  Seek GOD while he's here to be found. Pray to him while he's close at hand. Let the wicked abandon their way of life and the evil their way of thinking. Let them come back to GOD, who is merciful, come back to our God, who is lavish with forgiveness.

- **1 John 5:14-15**
  This is the confidence we have in approaching God: that if we **ask** anything according to his will, he hears us. And if we know that he **hears** us whatever we **ask,** we know that we have what we asked of him.

- **Jeremiah 29:12**
  Then you will call on me and come and pray to me, and I will **listen** to you.

ASSIGNMENT

Reflect on each of the above scriptures. Consider what you are currently doing to seek God and what you can do differently now to seek God more!

CHAPTER KEYS

1. God desires to communicate with us through prayer and wants us to seek after and consult him on the matters that are important to us. It is in the seeking that we get to truly know him and become sensitive to His voice.

2. Unconfessed sin separates us from God and hinders our prayers.

3. As you seek God, he will begin to show you the areas in your life and the things about you that are displeasing to him and keep you from possessing everything he has for you.

Prophetic Declarations Over Your Life

Whatever demonic assignment that is sent to kill, steal, destroy your life or your seed will be returned to the sender. Your kneading bowls, bank accounts, barns, and investments will overflow in abundance. You will grow in wisdom and stature just as Jesus did, and you shall have favor with both God and Man. Your cup will overflow in the abundance of prosperity, health, and resources. There will be no lack in any area of your life or your family's life. Everyone who encounters your presence shall be blessed in it. You and your family shall live and not die to declare the works of the only true and living God. In Jesus' name. Amen!

CHAPTER FOUR
DEVELOPING YOUR PRAYER LIFE

Consistency is a big part of having an effective prayer life. Try to find a quiet place and time that you can come before the Lord without distractions. A place that is accessible at all times just for you. The Word of God says that Jesus found a solitary place to pray. Solitary means to go to a *secluded* place, unfrequented, a lonely place where no one other than you is likely to be. Jesus shows us in Mark 1:35. Personal reflection and self-examination in one's solitary prayer time are essential. Developing your prayer life will take both commitment and dedication.

Confessing, declaring, and praying the Word of God is critical if you expect to see results. Make a list of scriptures and pray them daily. Habakkuk 2:2 says that we should write the vision and make it plain and that those who read it will run with it. I maintain what I call a "God Track." I adapted this method from Elder Yul (Jane) Crawford. A God track is a list of prayers or things that I request in the faith from God. As I list them, I indicate the date of my request and the scriptures used as a foundation for each prayer. By meditating on and studying the Word of God, we lay a foundation of biblical principles and promises that will establish God's will for our lives and circumstances. First, pray the prayer, secondly, write the prayer out, and thirdly, thank God for answering it in advance. Understand that God hears us the first time we pray. Once God answers the prayer, go ahead and write the date beside your prayer request as a sign of victory. This serves as a testimonial reminder of what our God has done. You can review them as a reminder that God will and can do it again in challenging moments.

I learned these basic principles from one of the elders at a church I formerly attended. I began to do the same. Later, the Lord would reveal additional principles to use in keeping a God track. He began to show me that if I added the date that he answered the prayer, this was a sign of victory. I soon learned the power of God in a new way through prayer. When I found myself in a place of uncertainty, the Holy Spirit would bring back to my remembrance my victories and show me that God does answer prayer. Keeping a God track will serve as a sign of memorial in your life, and it becomes a legacy or inheritance to your children's children. According to Proverbs 13:22, a good man leaves an inheritance to his children's children. Before us, the generations would pass down their history through quilts made from their ancestor's clothing, while others told their history by cutting and marking on tree rings.

As we proceed in developing an effective prayer life, we need to understand a few terms involved in prayer. Tyndale's definition of prayer means to address God with adoration, confession, supplication or thanksgiving, to intercede. Adoration expresses deep love and respect. Confession simply means to declare, an expression of faith, or to reveal sins. Supplication is the act of asking, pleading, or begging, earnestly requesting of God in reference to a need, desire, or something else. Thanksgiving is the expression of gratitude toward

God. To intercede means to go before God intervening on behalf of someone else. (Oxford Dictionary)

At the end of each year, I take time to reflect over the current year and evaluate what is working in my life and what needs to go, change, or adjust. I ask myself if these things have any real benefit or should I stop. Does it make a difference in my life or those who are in my life? For years, I was a stay-at-home mom. There was a strong desire in my heart to raise my children in the home. I wanted to give them a great start, a solid foundation, and a sense of family. Family has always been very important to me. If you ask the people in my inner circle, what is the most important thing in my life, they will say her family? One of my greatest fears was not to have a family or a sense of belonging. Everyone wants to feel that they are loved, wanted, and belong to something. There was a time when I had to separate my family, our priorities, and myself over attending church functions. I received a call from one of my ministry leaders requesting that I attend a meeting. It was a very important meeting. Once I told the leader I would not be able to attend, the conversation went downhill. The leader gave me all the reasons why I should be there, and I finally said that I have other priorities at this time, and I just cannot make it. I struggled with this so badly until I called one of my mentors at the time for guidance. Her response to me was there is going to come a time when all of your children will be grown and will not require as much out of you as they do now. Your calling is to your home first, and everything else will fall into place.

As I write the contents of this book, some of those children are now grown. I guess she was right. I smell freedom just around the corner! I adapted this principle to every area of my life. God, family, and whatever fits in. Every intercessor, watchman on the wall, prayer warrior, minister of music, dancer, teacher, etc., has his or her own assignment in the Body of Christ. By collectively working together, we will all accomplish God's will where praying is concerned. Never compare your assignment to anyone else. Use your gift so that it will make room for you.

Growing up, my family was not any different from anyone or anybody else's. On my mom's side of the family, we had our granny, her two sisters, her brothers, and numerous cousins. Each year one of my aunts called the family together for holidays, and all of the other sisters and their families would come together to celebrate. The uncles and their families showed up as well. Those were the good old days. One of my aunts never took no for an answer. Each had their own assignment, and none of them overstepped their boundaries. One of my aunts made her famous cake. It did not matter how many she made. It never seemed as if it was enough. The other sister would make her famous deviled eggs and special side dishes. My granny would drive several hours just to get there, and when she and my granddad opened the trunk of their car, it was full of our favorite foods; Gumbo, red beans and rice, cake, oranges from my granddad's trees, all kinds of treats and a special something for all of the grandkids. Everyone's favorite uncle would be somewhere cleaning. I also enjoyed spending time with my dad's side of the family, as well. They blended in with my mom's side of the family and supported us whenever they could. I took a moment to mention this because building any type of relationship or foundation requires time, effort, and a lot of work. My family is not perfect, but we're still family.

Everyone has their own gifts, talents, and calling. The Body of Christ is made up of all types of people, each with their own gift. These gifts will make room for you in your God given assignment and bring you before great men. Remember that it is God who ordains every person for his assigned purpose.

FURTHER STUDY

- 1 Peter 4:7
- 2 Chronicles 7:14 -15
- Colossians 4:2
- Daniel 6:10
- Psalm 5:2
- Romans 12:12

EXERCISE

On a scale of 1 to 5, with 1 being the least and 5 being the greatest, how much time do you spend on the following? Be honest. Is this a heart issue that stands between you and God? How much does this affect how much time you spend in the Word of God, for yourself, or with your families? Are these things causing issues in your personal life? God created the family before he created anything else in your life. Read Genesis 1:7-25. If none of what I have listed in this section needs revamping, you are doing great. However, feel free to add to it.

Church   1◯   2◯   3◯   4◯   5◯

Exercising 1◯   2◯   3◯   4◯   5◯

Going to every church function out of fear or obligation 1◯ 2◯ 3◯ 4◯ 5◯

Outreach programs 1◯   2◯   3◯   4◯   5◯

Reflecting on who you truly are & your assignment 1○ 2○ 3○ 4○ 5○

School functions 1○ 2○ 3○ 4○ 5○

Serving in the church 1○ 2○ 3○ 4○ 5○

Serving on different boards or committees 1○ 2○ 3○ 4○ 5○

Shopping 1○ 2○ 3○ 4○ 5○

Social Media 1○ 2○ 3○ 4○ 5○

Sorority or fraternity meeting 1○ 2○ 3○ 4○ 5○

Spending time with yourself 1○ 2○ 3○ 4○ 5○

Talking on the phone 1○ 2○ 3○ 4○ 5○

Watching TV 1○ 2○ 3○ 4○ 5○

Working 1○ 2○ 3○ 4○ 5○

_____ 1○ 2○ 3○ 4○ 5○

_____ 1○ 2○ 3○ 4○ 5○

What keeps you from spending time in the Word of God and prayer?

_____

_____

_____

How do you handle these distractions? _____

_____

_____

Is this really a distraction or an excuse? _____

_____

_____

When was the last time you really sought-after God with your whole heart, mind, spirit and soul? _____

_____

_____

Do you really seek the kingdom of God and its righteousness first so that all things will be added unto you? _____

_____

_____

Who or what is a distraction in your life that you need to place boundaries on? Why have you not done this? _____

_____

_____

Do you get enough rest so that you can put the work in? _____

_____

_____

IN THIS MANNER PRAY

Daily confessing your prayer requests in faith, standing firmly on God's Word will produce for you. Specifically, Isaiah 55:11 states, "So is my word that goes out from my mouth: It will not return to me empty, but will accomplish what I desire and achieve the purpose for which I sent it." Take God at His Word and watch Him do great and mighty things for you through your committed prayer life!

ASSIGNMENT

Start in prayer and meditation. Make a list of your concerns, what you're facing, current circumstances, along with the things that you are trusting/believing God to do in any area of your life. Use this as a basis to start your own God track and prayer devotional. After laying a foundation in prayer, search the Word of God as a foundation to build upon. Always write the date of your prayer request and God's answer to your prayer as a remembrance of God's faithfulness to answer your prayers. Always remember to take time to show God both gratitude and thanks for hearing and answering your prayers. Now let's **Watch God Move**!

Here is a sample of a **God Track**. Let us start here. Answer each question. Additional God Tracks are located in the back of this book.

DATE:_____

What am I facing today? _____

_____

48 | P a g e

_____

_____

What does scripture say about this situation/circumstance? Use scripture as a foundation to build your prayer request. _____

_____

_____

Prayer Request_____

_____

_____

Foundational Scriptures_____

_____

_____

Prayer of Gratitude and Thanks_____

_____

_____

What am I thankful for?_____

_____

_____

Praise Moment_____

_____

_____

Ask yourself, did I pray for someone else or their circumstances?

_____

_____

_____

PRAYER ANSWERED DATE: _____

Remember to write how God answered your request and share your testimony with only those whom God leads you to. Pray with a *purpose* and for a purpose. Find someone that you can call from time to time and asked them how you can pray for them and support them in this area.

What We Can Learn from The Prayer Life of Jesus

Hebrews 5:7 ERV gives us foundational text on how Jesus prayed, lived a life of prayer, and his accomplishments in prayer. It reads as follows, "While Jesus was here on earth, he offered prayers and pleadings with a loud cry and tears, to the one who could rescue him from death and God heard his prayers because of his deep reverence for God."

Most of us grew up hearing Bible stories on the life of Jesus; what he did for us on Calvary. We heard of the awesome miracles, signs, and wonders that followed him but never heard much about his prayer life. Let me reiterate this,

Jesus had a meaningful and devoted prayer life. There is no way he could hear the voice of God as clearly as he did or keep and finish his God-given assignments without it. Jesus prayed for our salvation, safety, and assignments before we were born, and while we were yet sinners, operating outside of the will of God for our lives. Isaiah 53:12b says He was counted among the rebels. He bore the sins of many and interceded for rebels. Oxford's dictionary defines *rebel* as a person who rises in opposition or armed resistance against an established government. As a matter of fact, while you are reading this book, he is making intercession on your behalf to the Father. Read Romans 8:34 and write it out in the space provided. _____

_____

_____

Jesus Prays for the Believers

John 17 states that Jesus prayed for the believers past, present, and future. He asked God to make us one with Him just as he and Jesus were one. He mentioned to God that he did not lose one of those he gave to him, not even the one destined for destruction. Take a moment to read the entire chapter. Once you have finished, reflect upon the scriptures and draw a line under those that speak directly to you. In the space provided, reflect and write out a response to what speaks to you.

_____

_____

_____

_____

_____

_____

Jesus' prayer serves as a reminder of how much he loves us and wants a relationship with us. He thought so much of us that he sent a prayer reminder to God on their relationship, his assignments being fulfilled, and every step Jesus took prior to going to the cross on our behalf. Here Jesus is reminding God that his time had come, reminding God that he was heading to the finale. He was going to the cross, but before he embarked on his final journey to the cross, he said, dad, remember this. Let's take a look at how this chapter breaks down. After reading each section, meditate, reflect, pray, and complete each section's follow-up questions.

> **John 17: 1-6 (ERV)** After saying all these things, Jesus looked up to heaven and said, "Father, the hour has come. Glorify to your Son so he can give glory back to you. ² For you have given him authority over everyone. He gives eternal life to each one you have given him. ³And this is the way to have eternal life to know you, the only true God, and Jesus Christ, the one you sent to earth. ⁴ I brought glory to you here on earth by completing the work you gave me to do. ⁵ Now, Father, bring me into the glory we shared before the world began.⁶ "I have revealed you to the ones you gave me from this world. They were always yours. You gave them to me, and they have kept your Word.

Prayer

Lord, as we meditate on these scriptures today, we ask that you would guide us by your Holy Spirit of truth. Let us experience your glory. Be glorified in us and through us. Teach us to number our days and to use wisdom and discretion as we go about our day. Wrap your loving arms around us. Send your comforter to bring comfort to those who are grieving. Bring healing to those who need healing. We cover ourselves, families, colleagues, the body of Christ, and those with whom we have a relationship with in the blood of Jesus. We apply this prayer to everyone's life in Jesus' name. Amen

Reflections

What do you think that Jesus meant by asking God to glorify him?

_____

_____

_____

What does it mean to glorify God?_____

_____

_____

_____

Is there any area in your life that God is not glorified in? _____

_____

_____

John 17: 7-8 (ERV) 7 Now they know that everything I have is a gift from you, 8 for I have passed on to them the message you gave me. They accepted it and know that I came from you, and they believe you sent me.

As we meditate on this passage of scripture, we learn that Jesus is praying for the believers and is sending a reminder to God on our behalf that he reveals him to the ones God had assigned to him. My question today is, have you made known to God that you are aware of those that have been assigned to you and that you are committed to your assignments? God has given each of us an assignment to make known to him. Are we revealing who he is to others, sharing the gospel of Jesus Christ, or keeping our walks undercover for fear of what others may think of us? Not certain how to accomplish this? Let us move forward today by bringing true revelation of who God really is to others. Share what he has done in your life. It's time. Stop waiting on others to release you into ministry. God ordained you before the foundation of the world, and Jesus commissioned you to go into all of the earth to proclaim the gospel. You've got your marching orders. Now get moving!

Prayer

Lord, teach us to reveal who you are to those you have assigned to us. Show us who they are and what our true assignment is in their lives. Reveal yourself to us. Help us to walk with them, and be an encouragement to them. In Jesus' name, amen.

John 17: 9-12 (ERV) [9] "My prayer is not for the world, but for those you have given me, because they belong to you. [10] All who are mine belong to you, and you have given them to me, so they bring me glory. [11] Now I am departing from the world; they are staying in this world, but I am coming to you. Holy Father, you have given me your name; now protect them by the power of your name so that they will be united just as we are. [12] During my time here, I protected them by the power of the name you gave me. I guarded them so that not one was lost, except the one headed for destruction, as the scriptures foretold.

Reflections

How should we pray for the world? _____

_____

_____

Who has God entrusted you to disciple? _____

_____

_____

Are you committed enough to pray for them consistently? _____

_____

_____

Are they truly prepared to carry on their assignment? _____

_____

_____

How are you praying for them? _____

_____

_____

Prayer

Heavenly Father, thank you for protecting us by your name! Thank you that not one of us will be lost. Thank you that even though we are in the world, we're not a part of it and for keeping us safe in it. Lord, bring us closer to you and continue to reveal to us the mysteries of your kingdom. Thank you for your Son, Jesus Christ, and for all that you did through him to reveal your glory to us and through us and for those who are to come in his name and by your power. In Jesus' name, amen.

John 17: 13-19 (ERV) 13 "Now I am coming to you. I told them many things while I was with them in this world so they would be filled with my joy. 14 I have given them your word. And the world hates them because they do not belong to the world, just as I do not belong to the world. 15 I'm not asking you to take them out of the world, but to keep them safe from the evil one. 16 They do not belong to this world any more than I do. 17 Make them holy by your truth; teach them your word, which is truth. 18 Just as you sent me into the world, I am sending them into the world. 19And I give myself as a holy sacrifice for them so they can be made holy by your truth.

Reflections

Are you comfortable with sharing who Christ is? _____

_____

_____

How are you sharing the Word of God with others? _____

_____

_____

Does God's word stand true to you? _____

_____

_____

Are you able to define yourself against the world by using the Word of God?

_____

_____

_____

Where does our protection come from? _____

_____

_____

Prayer

Lord, we receive your word; we know that your word is true. Thank you for protecting us from the things of this world and for revealing your truth to us through your son Jesus Christ. We know that the Word became flesh and dwelt among us. Thank you that we can run to you and find safety in your word and in you. You are our greatest protector, and no matter what we face, we know that you are with us and will carry us until Christ returns. We find complete joy in knowing who you are and in knowing your son Jesus the Christ. In Jesus' name, amen.

John 17: 20-23 (ERV) [20] "I am praying not only for these disciples but also for all who will ever believe in me through their message. [21] I pray that they will all be one, just as you and I are one—as you are in me, Father, and I am in you. And may they be in us so that the world will believe you sent me. [22] "I have given them the glory you gave me, so they may be one as we are one. [23] I am in them, and you are in me. May they experience such perfect unity that the world will know that you sent me and that you love them as much as you love me.

Reflections

Take a moment to thank God for allowing Jesus to pray for you, his disciple. In the above passage of scripture who does Jesus pray for and how does he pray for them? _____

_____

_____

What makes us one with Christ? _____

_____

_____

Prayer

Lord, we thank you that Jesus prayed for us as future disciples and that others would believe in you because of our message, our testimony, and lifestyles. Please forgive us for every time we did not honor you or keep your word and did not display Christlike behaviors. Father, there were times in our lives where we failed to bring you glory by disobeying your word. Because of this, you were not glorified. Reveal those areas in our lives where we're not bringing you glory and give us the grace that we need to walk it out. Lord, make us one with you and Jesus as he prayed. Father, your word says that two cannot walk unless they agree. We seek you today and asked that you make us one with you and Jesus, just as he prayed. In Jesus' name, amen.

> **John 17:24-26 (ERV)** [24] Father, I want these whom you have given me to be with me where I am. Then they can see all the glory you gave me because you loved me even before the world began! [25] "O righteous Father, the world doesn't know you, but I do; and these disciples know you sent me. [26] I have revealed you to them, and I will continue to do so. Then your love for me will be in them, and I will be in them."

Reflections

Why was Jesus praying this way? _____

_____

_____

Where was he planning to go? _____

_____

_____

Are we truly sitting in heavenly places with Christ Jesus? _____

_____

_____

Prayer

Lord, thank you for hearing our prayers and for allowing us to see that Jesus prayed for us before we were born and before we knew who you were for ourselves. Lord, we pray for the people who you called to disciple us even when we were not ready to receive your message. Thank you for every person who did not give up on us and for those who you called to demonstrate your love, your power, and sovereignty. Lord, please continue to reveal to us who you truly are and help us to reveal both you and Christ to the world, to our families, and those whom you have assigned to us. In Jesus' name, amen.

FURTHER STUDY

- Luke 22:39-44
- Luke 4:21 -22
- Luke 9:28- 30
- Mark 1:35

 CHAPTER KEYS

1. Developing an effective prayer life is more about our relationship with God than about getting what we want. It requires time and commitment. It requires honesty in our hearts.

2. Keeping track of the prayers God has answered encourages us in times of great trial and frustration. It strengthens our faith to know God is more than able to handle our current matters because he has a track record of answering your prayers!

3. Jesus teaches us the importance of praying for others regardless of our feelings towards an individual. We are to pray for God's will to be done in their life.

Prophetic Declarations Over Your Life

Your relationships are blessed, whole, healthy, complete, and lacking nothing. You shall praise the Lord in spirit and in truth. Your testimonies shall bless others; man will see and tell of God's glorious works in heaven. You are an overcomer by the blood of the Lamb and the word of your testimony. God will extend his grace to you. He will continually extend his kindness to you and your family throughout all generations. You shall look for your enemies in vain. Your angry enemies will be scattered and humiliated. Nothing by any means shall harm you. In the day of adversity, God will hide you in his secret tabernacle. When others are faced with doom, misfortune, or calamity, it will not touch you. You and your family shall be a beacon of light unto everyone you encounter. Misfortune will not be your portion. The Lord, your God, will increase you and your children more and more. In Jesus' name, amen!

CHAPTER FOUR
PRAY IN THE NAME OF JESUS

Jesus gave us permission to "name drop" him, to use his name on our behalf with unlimited or infinite use. His name has power and gives us authority over the powers of darkness. This isn't the only reason we use his name. Jesus is the mediator between both God and man. Jesus sets at the right hand of God the Father and is making intercession on our behalf. Since Jesus' current posture is sitting at the right of God the Father, we have instant, unhindered, and immediate access to the Father. In other words, God sees Jesus, not us, not our sin, not our past. God sees us through the eyes of Jesus and his redemptive work on the cross.

Once you truly understand the power that comes from using the name of Jesus, God will unveil his hidden power to you. We have all heard of the works Jesus did while on the earth. He even said that we would do greater works than him. These works won't be revealed without our spending time in prayer. Jesus' name causes sick bodies to be healed, transforms lives, causes demons to flee, makes people walk in new levels of self-worth, and gives many confidence and value. There is no other name that we can pray through or pray in that God will

IN THIS MANNER PRAY

hear and answer. Take this personally. Jesus, unlike man, wants you to use his name and benefit from it.

Scripture References

- John 14:6
- John 14:13
- John 14:14

While shopping in a local retail store one day, I came across a poster with the names of Jesus on it. It caught my attention. As I stood there, I made a conscious decision to purchase it. I later had it framed. I wanted to have it in a place that I would frequently pass. This would help me memorize and apply them in prayer as I walked around the house. Developing simple strategies such as this keeps you focused and helps you grow. Growing up, we were taught if it's important to you, you will remember it. Many of us grew up writing out what we deemed important. We would put it on a calendar or tape it to the refrigerator. I keep a note pad near my bed and on my desk to make sure I remember what is important.

Who Is Jesus?

You may find this to be a strange question, but if you're going to be using someone's name, you should probably know who they are and what qualifies their name to have the kind of authority that scares demons! Jesus' name is defined as a teacher of the Jewish religion. His life, death, and resurrection are the basis by which all men are saved. (Merriam-Webster Dictionary). Jesus' name

64 | P a g e

and meaning were revealed to his mother Mary, through the angel Gabriel in Luke 1:31-33.   The book of Isaiah 9:6-7 lays a foundation of who Jesus is and what Jesus would become to God's chosen people. It reads as follows," For a child is born to us, a son is given to us. The government will rest on his shoulders. And he will be called: Wonderful Counselor, Mighty God, Everlasting Father, Prince of Peace. His government and its peace will never end. He will rule with fairness and justice from the throne of his ancestor David for all eternity. The passionate commitment of the LORD of Heaven's Armies will make this happen!"

Let's take some time to study who Jesus is to us. Jesus' names give us an infinite description of who he really is. Scripture tells us that there was nothing special about his outer appearance; however, it does share with us that his garments were seamless.

- Jesus is *Our Redeemer:* Redeemer, by definition, is the purchasing of something that was lost. We were lost before we came to the knowledge and power of Jesus Christ.

  > **Job 19:25** He was sent by God to be our sacrificial lamb. His sacrifice through his shed blood covered all of our sins. Because of this act of love, we are rightly restored to God before the first Adam sinned and caused us to be born into sin.

- Jesus is *Our Healer*. I am reminded of the blind man on the side of the road who needed healing (John 9:1-42). He heals a man at the Pool of Bethesda

(John 5:1-13). During this encounter, Jesus asked a man who had been sitting by the pool for a very long time, patiently waiting for someone to put him in the water so he could be healed. Jesus simply asked this young man if he wanted to be healed. No excuses, just a simple answer, do you want to be healed. Then Jesus gave him three commands: get up, take your mat, and walk out of this. What situation are you currently facing? Know that Jesus has asked, "Do you want to be healed from this?" Are you willing to take up your mat and walk away? Jesus healed the women with the issue of blood (Mark 5:25-34). He also redeemed the lady who was caught in adultery (Matthew 5:27-30). While her accusers stood armed with stones and ready to stone her for the act she committed, Jesus asked one simple question, "Which one of you has never sinned?" No one could answer him. He said, go ahead and cast your stone if you're free from sin. All of her accusers left.

- Jesus is *Our Deliverer*. He carries the sins of the world, and our government is upon his shoulder. Isaiah 9:6 Deliver, according to biblehub.com, is to be set free from restraint, to liberate, rescued from evil. Christ delivered humanity from the sins they committed and empowered us to be free from everything that keeps us from experiencing God's forgiveness and freedom.

- Jesus is *Our Intercessor*, constantly making or interceding on our behalf (Romans 8:26-34). An intercessor is a person who intervenes on behalf of others, especially by prayer (Oxford Dictionary). Jesus prayed for each of us in John 17. The scripture clearly tells us that he is currently making intercession on behalf.

Here are a few other names for Christ revealed in the Bible. After reading this, consider who Jesus is to you. You may want to write each of these scripture references out and commit them to memory. By doing this, you will develop a better sense of who Jesus is and what he did for our lives.

- Immanuel - God with us. (Isaiah 7:14 & Matthew 1:23)
- Teacher and Lord (John 13:13)
- Master (Matthew 8:19)
- Savior (John 4:42)
- Rose of Sharon (Songs of Solomon 2:1)
- The Way...Truth...The Life (John 14:6)
- Prince of Peace (Isaiah 9:6)

ASSIGNMENT

To me, Jesus is my savior and my redeemer. Before totally surrendering to God, I did not know this. I knew of it, but not that it applied to my life. Knowing that Jesus sacrificed his life for me personally is totally different from him being the savior of the world. Every work he did while he resided on the earth covers every person who accepts him as Lord and savior.

There were times when I found myself in certain situations that I just began to simply say, "Jesus, I need you! This is what I am facing. I know that by your name, sick bodies are healed, and I experienced healing, deliverance, and hope." Take some time to meditate and reflect upon the names of Jesus and ask yourself, do I really know Jesus and who He is. Have I benefited from who Jesus is and what he has done in my life?

Jesus is our High Priest (Hebrews 9:11-28)

We know that we are no longer under the old covenant of worship because Christ was the ultimate sacrifice that mediated a new covenant. Under this new covenant, does God still have a required place of Worship? Is there still a Holy Place for God to be received in the earth? Verse 12 says that Christ entered "the Most Holy Place once and for all and secured OUR redemption forever." Christ's blood was shed one time for all of humanity and will never shed again. Unlike the animal sacrifices of old that require all of these different animals presented based on their sin.

What are the benefits of this new covenant? We no longer need a Priest to offer any sacrifices on our behalf or to mediate between God and man. Christ resolved this issue. Once we accepted Jesus Christ as our Lord and Savior, we entered into this new covenant, and it can't be revoked unless we relinquish it. Once Christ redeemed humanity, he returned to the Father, took his rightful place, and is seated in Heavenly places giving us a permanent Mediator and instant access to the Father through him. No more daily animal sacrifices in hopes of sins being forgiven. No longer relying on the priest to make atonement, praying that the High Priest did not have any hidden sins in his life that would cause his death and your sins pending or hanging in the balance. No more blood

IN THIS MANNER PRAY

being sprinkled around an altar, eagerly awaiting forgiveness. No more carrying animals on your back or pulling up to the House of God with all kinds of animals in your car, hoping you could get them to the priest or, into today's world, your pastor. Some of us would need a car so big until we might just leave out some animals in hopes that no one would notice how many sins we committed since the last time and offering was made.

Growing up in the Catholic Church, I would go to the priest before mass and confess my sins to the priest. I would ask the priest to forgive me of my sins and confess that I had sinned since my last confession. The priest would then pray for me and tell me how many *Our Fathers* and *Hail Marys* I needed to pray. I can be totally honest. I became so bored at this point in my life until I can't even remember if I ever finished them all. This is not mentioned to point out or bash any of my upbringing. I mentioned this to show you that our new covenant under Christ redeem this. As a people, we sometimes confess our sins but fail to repent from them. Confession and repentance are equally important.

As a result, we no longer need a priest to confess our sins. We can ask for forgiveness of our sins. Remember that Christ is constantly making intercession on our behalf. What a great exchange. We will conclude by reflecting on verses 24-28 reflecting on the goodness of our God and what he, along with Christ, has done for our families and us. Take a moment to highlight what Christ has done and meditate on it as you go about your day. Thank God for our eternal High Priest.

69 | P a g e

Memory Scriptures

- **Hebrew 5:1** Every high priest is a man chosen to represent other people in their dealings with God. He presents their gifts to God and offers sacrifices for their sins.

- **Hebrews 11-12** So Christ has now become the High Priest over all the good things that have come. He has entered that greater, more perfect Tabernacle in heaven, which was not made by human hands and is not part of this created world. With his own blood—not the blood of goats and calves—he entered the Most Holy Place once for all time and secured our redemption forever.

Prayer Demonstrations

Father God, I come to you in the name of Jesus, and I ask that you heal me by the stripes of Jesus. Cleanse me with the blood of Jesus and make me whole just as you did for the woman with the issue of blood. Lord, your word says that you would supply my every need according to his riches in glory by your son Christ Jesus. I need _____. I stand in expectation of my needs, desires, and wants being fulfilled this day. Your word says that Jesus exchanged his riches for my property. Your word even says that you already know what I need before I ask. Prove your word as truth and make it evident of who you are in my life. In Jesus' name. Amen.

In the name of Jesus, I petition your throne of grace that _____ find mercy today. Have mercy on them. Heal, set free, and deliver. Lord, you are not willing that _____ perishes but comes to repentance. Give them a heart of repentance. I know that your word says that no one can come to you unless your Spirit draws them. So, I ask you in the name of Jesus to draw them by your Spirit. In Jesus' name, amen!

 **CHAPTER KEYS**

1. Use the name of Jesus that applies to your situation.

2. It is God's desire that his will be done. Let your will go so that he can accomplish the works in you and in others.

3. Remember to set aside some time to meditate on the Word of God so that you are strengthened when needed.

Prophetic Declarations Over Your Life

Your family is blessed in their going in and in their going out. You have been redeemed from the curse of man and your past. Everything that was stolen, lost, or taken from you or your family shall be restored seven times more. You and your family are the head and are not the tail. Your family is above only and not beneath. God's faithfulness is extended throughout all of your generations, and his mercy will endure to your family forever. In Jesus' name, amen!

CHAPTER FIVE

YOU HAVE BEEN CHOSEN FOR THIS ASSIGNMENT

The word of the Lord, according to John 15:16, says, " You did not choose me, but I chose you and appointed you so that you might go and bear fruit—fruit that will last—and so that whatever you ask in my name the Father will give you." Chosen means to be set apart, selected, preferred, or given special consideration. Matthew 22:14 states that many are called, but few are chosen. Romans 9:11-12 says before they were born, before they did anything good or bad, she meaning Rebekah received a message from God in reference to her twins. This message confirms that God chooses people for his own purposes. God calls people not based on what they have done, who they are, their parents, their family, or their choices, be it good, bad, or indifferent.

1 Peter 2:9 says, "For you are a chosen people; a royal priesthood and a holy nation, God's special possession." God chooses imperfect people, people who come from all different backgrounds, without consulting any of them. He

chose Mordecai to raise Esther, who went from peasant girl to the Queen. While many thought Esther was being groomed to be a queen. God was calling her to lead her people. Esther's submission to Mordecai's demands when he heard that Haman was going to have their people put to death caused her to make a conscious decision. If I perish, I perish. Esther called her people to a national fast as they prepared for battle. Not only did she take Haman down, but an entire nation.

Moses was drawn from the water after being hidden because his mom refused to let him be killed at the hand of Pharaoh's command. He lived in the king's palace, was raised by the king's daughter, learned the Egyptian language, overheard the conversations about his people, saw their oppression, ran for his life, and later received his marching orders from the Lord to tell Pharaoh to let God's people go. From a basket of water to the leader of the Israelites.

At that time, the Hebrew midwives were handpicked by Pharaoh to kill all of the males born to the Israelites. Since they refused to kill the male children, they were called in by Pharaoh to account for the children's births. The midwives feared God and responded, "They aren't like the Hebrew women. By the time we get to them, they have already given birth." The midwives' obedience to God invoked God to bless them by giving their own children. They went from midwives to moms. I could go on in great detail, Sampson, John the Baptist, Hannah, Job, your parents, and even you. Understand that you were chosen, handpicked, selected without any say for this assignment. God has a purpose for you to fulfill as an intercessor.

An intercessor is someone who stands in the place of another and prays on their behalf. The life of an intercessor is selfless. Often, it seems as if your life doesn't belong to you. It can be very sacrificial, leading to sleepless nights, broken sleep, etc. I can remember a time where it appeared that my days were off. I was barely sleeping. I had a small child, a newborn, and a one-year-old baby. Needless to say, the newborn and the one-year-old had different sleeping patterns. One would be asleep, and the other one would be up. Couple this with a 5 a.m. prayer life and a 7 a.m. carpool, it seemed like I couldn't get it together, and I had help with my children. After the children went to bed one night, I prayed, and this is what I said. Lord, if you want me to come before you in the morning, these babies will need to sleep all night. I can't nurse, get up and down all throughout the night and come before you. That night, both of those babies slept all night. I couldn't believe it. I slept with one eye open, waiting on one of them to wake up. Can you say thank you, Jesus? From that night on, they slept, and I was able to make it to my prayer closet.

To understand your assignment, you must know what an intercessor or intercession is. Oxford defines it as a person who intervenes on behalf of another, especially in prayer. Wikipedia defines intercession or intercessory prayer as the act of praying to a deity on behalf of others. Jesus is the best example that we have concerning intercession, according to John 17. Romans 8:3 clearly states that Christ Jesus is the one who died and was raised for us and is sitting at the right hand of God interceding for us. Christ didn't merely assume himself to be our High Priest. God chose him for the position as revealed by Hebrews 5:4-5.

ASSIGNMENT

Ask yourselves who has God asked you to pray and intercede for? Create a list of people, places, issues, family concerns, community, or nation that God assigned to you to pray for. How can you apply the Word of God to the situation? Are you prepared to pray in this area until you are released from the assignment or until a resolution manifests?

_____

_____

_____

_____

_____

 CHAPTER KEYS

1. Being obedient to God will invoke God's blessing upon you.

2. God has a purpose for you to fulfill as an intercessor. You are the only person who can complete your assignment.

3. God chose you.

Prophetic Declarations Over Your Life

You shall bless others because you have been abundantly blessed. According to his riches in glory, the Lord will supply all of your needs by Christ Jesus. You are connected to every person you need to walk out your destiny, and you shall fulfill your destiny in Christ Jesus. God's plan is to give you a future and hope. He will bring you to his expected end. You and your household shall walk in the things of God, keeping his covenant throughout all generations. You will destroy the works of the devil, and the evil one will not touch you. In Jesus' name, amen!

CHAPTER SIX

SPIRITUAL WEAPONS FOR EFFECTIVE PRAYERS

The Bible tells us that we have spiritual weapons, and we are to war with them in prayer. We use these God-given mighty weapons, not worldly weapons, to pull down the strongholds of human reasoning and to destroy false arguments standing up against the knowledge of God. We destroy every proud obstacle that keeps people from knowing God. We take authority over rebellious thoughts and bring them into obedience to Christ. (2 Corinthians 10:4-6).

Remember that we do not wrestle against flesh and blood. The enemy, meaning Satan, is your true enemy, not the people whom we're at odds with. Note to self, anyone who rubs you the wrong way is either being used by God or the devil. Learn the difference. I have encountered some people in life that I never want to encounter again. Some people may feel the same toward me, but in the end, I came to realize that they were on their assignment. When you are a fighter by nature, this can be very hard. God is only fine-tuning those areas in your life that don't bring him glory. God wants us to understand that true battles and victories are won in the spiritual realm. Let's work on sharpening our weapons. What exactly are some of those spiritual weapons?

The Blood of Jesus

Pleading the blood commands the works that were done on the cross by Jesus to manifest on your behalf. The blood of Jesus cancels the assignment of the enemy on your life, the lives of family, friends, loved ones, and so forth. The name of Jesus causes both your enemies and demons to flee. Allow me to reiterate: There is power in the Name and Blood of Jesus! Plead means to present, argue in a place of position in court or public; to make an emotional appeal as defined by Oxford Dictionaries.

Bind and Loose

Bind means to tie down with great constraint or to tighten as tight as possible. This ensures that it will not come open. Loose, in simple terms, means the opposite. When something is loosed, it is easily detached or released from. Those are the things you don't want to hold on to. In prayer, we are given the right and authority to bind the devil's evil works and his demonic forces that were intended to cause harm to other individuals or us. We have the authority to lose ourselves and others from every circumstance that attempts to destroy us. By doing so, we destroy Satan and his tactics. For example: *I bind the demonic activity plaguing this region or territory, and I lose the angels of God to destroy every evil plan and scheme that comes with it. Its plague will not destroy the people of God or their seed. In Jesus' name, I destroy the works of the devil through the blood of Jesus. Every demon cease from your evil works. Lord dispatch the angels you have assigned over this region or territory to do warfare on its behalf. I release love, peace, healing, freedom, etc. In Jesus' name, amen.*

Read *Matthew 18:18 NLT. I tell you the truth, whatever you forbid on earth will be forbidden in heaven, and whatever you permit on earth will be permitted in heaven.*

As we operate our weapons in prayer, we must be mindful to pray without ceasing. When we communicate with God through prayer, we give God a vessel to use to pray His that will on the earth be done. If no one is praying for His will, how can God's will be released on earth? Therefore, as God's chosen people, we cannot stop praying as long as there is breath in our bodies! Meditate on the following scriptures.

- **1 Thessalonians 5:17**
  Rejoice and give thanks no matter what happens or how long it takes.

- **Luke 18:1**
  Men ought to always pray and not to faint.

- **Romans 12:12**
  Be joyful in hope, patient in affliction, faithful in prayer.

Matthew 18:19. I also tell you this: *If two of you agree here on earth concerning anything you ask, my Father in heaven will do it for you. For where two or three gather together as my followers, I am there among them.* There is power in agreement. Every one of us needs other people in our lives to help us in our daily walk with God, in our personal lives, and in our prayer life. There are times in our lives when we have things coming at us from every area, and we need someone to cover us in the midst of what we're going through. Someone to help carry us. Always remember that the Holy Spirit inside of you can come into quick agreement with you. You may not always be able to reach your prayer partner.

God's Word Is Your Weapon

Using the Word of God as a weapon is very beneficial to your life. In Ephesians chapter 6, the Bible refers to the sword of the spirit, which is the Word of God. This is a part of the armor of God, which we will discuss a little later. When you apply the Word of God to your life or situation, you force the hand of God to move. Did you know that angels listen for, hearken to, and are dispatched at the command of God's word (Psalm 103:20)? "Hearken means to heed to the Word, to do something about it, and to let it really change you." (Daily Devotion www.raystedman.org).

Whatever we speak manifests and becomes our reality. Confessing the word daily changes your perspective first and then your outcome. When God's word lines up with what you are confessing, you get results. I have heard people say that you can't find a scripture for everything you go through. I beg to differ. The word says for sure, there is an end to a matter (Proverbs 23:18-20). It also says that the Lord will perfect that which concerns me. It even says that we don't know how to pray, but the Spirit makes intercession for us. Enough said. God's word is a lamp unto our feet and a light unto our paths. God has us covered through his word.

God's word is a strategic and effective weapon in your prayer arsenal. This is why when we pray, we must put God in remembrance of his word. For example, Lord God, you said no weapon fashioned or formed against me would prosper. Lord God, you said I'm the head and not the tail. Lord God, you said you've given your angels charge over me. This is how we swing our sword in prayer. I challenge you to write out the promises of God found in the scriptures and then daily confess them out loud several times and watch what happens. For example, when praying for salvation for your loved ones: the Lord is not slack in his promises as man counts slackness, not willing that any man should perish, but_____ (all) comes to repentance. Add the person's name here. It is by your mercies oh Lord that _____ hasn't been consumed. Your love brings _____ new mercies each day.

 When facing injustice or mistreatment. The Lord will fight against those who fight against me. You will contend against _____ because they are contending with me. Lord direct me in this process. Bring revelation in this situation. Lord you will even turn the heart and head of _____ (the king) in favor toward_____. By the stripes of Jesus _____ is healed. Turn the hand of my enemy in my favor. Whatever was meant for the evil will work out for the good of _____.

When my children were young, I would have them repeat certain scriptures after me as we prayed. We confessed these scriptures as we headed to school, traveled, or just ran errands. I wanted to teach them to apply the word to their life. One year one of them fell off of their bike and suffered from a contusion as a result of the accident. After being released from the hospital, and it was time to return to school, I became very concerned about his face because of the scarring. As we discussed going back to school, I asked him if he wanted to stay home or was he ok with returning. His words to me were, "Mom, I am fearfully and wonderfully made." I asked, "Where did you learn this?" He said, "At Church." That day was a defining moment and confirmed to me that basic principles lead to life learned lessons. The Lord's Word is mighty. It's like a two-edged sword. It pierces, it cuts, and remembers. His Word is Jesus in the flesh. It accomplishes what it has been commanded to do.

Praise As A Weapon

Praise arrives from the Latin word "pretium," which means price. (Pursuing Intimacy with God, intimacywithgod.com). We show God how much we value him by spending time with him, praising him, worshiping him, and by being obedient to him. I will praise the Lord with my whole heart. Praise commands the attention of the one you are honoring at the moment. How many times have you watched someone being honored or given an award of achievement? By the time the person finishes honoring them, they are smiling so hard, or tears are rolling down their faces. They're sitting at full attention with ears opened and listening to every statement being made. So, it is with the Father. We command his attention the very moment we began to sing praises, make melodies to his name, or just simply say hello, Father.

Genesis 29:16-30 gives an account of the birth of the children who were born to Jacob and Leah, married by default. Leah married to a man whose heart was not with her. His love was for her sister. At the birthing of each child, she names them based on what she was experiencing at that time. Leah conceives again and brought forth a man child, and she said I would praise the Lord. She named him Judah and gave birth again. Judah was one of the sons of Jacob from which the tribe of Judah derived. In earlier biblical times, whenever the Israelites went to battle, they sent the tribe of Judah first. Judah simply means praise. Your praise is a weapon of bold declaration against the enemy. It's saying I'm going to praise God even in the face of adversity because he inhabits the praises of his people. So, as I begin to praise God even in prayer, it begins to confuse my enemies, confronts my enemies, and invokes the presence of God.

How many times have we heard you have to praise your way out? Psalm 9:1-2 says *I will praise you, Lord, with all my heart; I will tell of all the marvelous things you have done. I will be filled with joy because of you. I will sing praises to your name, O most high.* We see in verse three, the psalmist says his enemies retreated, stumbled, and died because the Lord showed up. In the midst of your praises, God shows up. Praise opens the door for God to come in and have his way.

Where do we praise God according to scripture?

- We praise God in the sanctuary; praise him in the firmaments of His power. **Psalm 150:1**
- Praise him from the heavens! Praise him from the skies. **Psalm 148:1**
- Praise the Lord from the earth. **Psalm 141:7**

How do we praise God?

- Praise him with a blast of the ram's horn; praise him with a lyre and harp! **Psalm 150:3-5**
- Praise him with the tambourine and dancing; praise him with strings and flutes. Praise him with a clash of cymbals. **Psalm 150:4-5**
- Sing out your thanks to the Lord; sing praises to our God with a harp. **Psalm 147:7**

Who should praise the Lord?

- Let everything that breathes sing praise to the Lord! This means you. As long as you are able to breathe, praise the Lord. **Psalm 150: 6**
- Praise the name of the Lord! Praise him, you who serve the Lord, you who serve in the house of the Lord, in the courts of the house of the Lord, in the courts of the house of our God. **Psalm 135:1-2**

Why do we praise the Lord?

- Praise the Lord, for the Lord is good; celebrate the Lord with lovely music. **Psalm 135:3**
- Praise him for his mighty works; praise his unequaled greatness. **Psalm 150:6**
- Praise the Lord! For it is good to sing praises unto our God; for it is pleasant, and a song of praise is fitting. 3 He heals the brokenhearted and binds up their wombs. **Psalm 147:1-3**
- Yet you are holy, enthroned on the praises of Israel your people. **Psalm 22:3**

When do we praise the Lord?

We praise the Lord no matter what and at all times. Put praise in your mouth and on your lips. Most people, including the enemy, do not understand how your praises are coming forth, and everything around you is falling apart. Psalm 34:1-3 says, *"I will bless the LORD at all times; His praise shall continually be in my mouth. My soul will make its boast in the LORD; the humble will hear it and rejoice. O magnify the LORD with me, And let us exalt His name together."*

We praise God when we are headed to his house and when we receive our healing. *Acts 3:1-9: Now Peter and John went up together into the temple at the hour of prayer, being the ninth hour. And a certain man lame from his mother's womb was carried, whom they laid daily at the gate of the temple which is called Beautiful, to ask alms of them that entered into the temple; who seeing Peter and John about to go into the temple asked an alms. And Peter, fastening his eyes upon him with John, said, Look on us. And he gave heed unto them, expecting to receive something of them. Then Peter said, Silver and gold have I none; but such as I have give I thee: In the name of Jesus Christ of Nazareth rise up and walk. And he took him by the right hand, and lifted him up: and immediately his feet and ankle bones received strength. And he leaping up stood, and walked, and entered with them into the temple, walking, and leaping, and praising God. And all the people saw him walking and praising God:*

Praise God in advance for victory. Praise God in the promotion of every season of life. Praise God in the morning, evening, and afternoon. Praise God at midday. Praise God in the midst of battle. Praise God when others succeed.

Declarations

- The Lord is my strength and song, and He has become my salvation. He is my God, and I will praise him, my father's God, and I will exalt him. **Exodus 15:2**

- I will thank the Lord according to his righteousness, and I will sing praise to the name of the Lord Most High. **Psalm 7:17**

Worship As A Weapon

The definition of worship is used as a transitive verb which means, to honor or show reverence for as a divine being or supernatural power; to regard with great or extravagant respect, honor, or devotion, a celebrity worshipped by her fans; to perform or take part in worship or an act of worship. I believe that true authentic praise will lead to worship. Praise and worship are fraternal twins, and when operating together, they can lead you into the presence of God.

The Word of God declares that every living thing should praise God. However, not all men can worship the Lord. The prerequisite, according to John 4:24, says that God is a spirit and that those who worship him must worship him in spirit and in truth. Paul says in 1Timothy 2:8 that his desire is for men to pray everywhere, lifting up holy hands without wrath, contentiousness, or doubt. This is why it is so important that we confess, ask for forgiveness, and repent before we pray, allowing the Holy Spirit of God to cleanse us. As we tap into worship, there will be times when the Holy Spirit of God will begin to reveal to us what God is after in us. Some of these things have been hard to swallow from my personal experience, while others I could easily release. Worship takes us into a place of holy reverence for God. True authentic worship not only leads you into the presence of God but is the place where God reveals himself to you. He reveals to you that secret part of him that only you and he can understand and comprehend. Worship allows you to tap into the side of God that you need the most at that time. Worship leads to healing, intimacy, and transparency. Worship becomes a powerful prayer weapon because it requires us to completely yield over to the Spirit of God. It is an act of surrender, saying unto the Lord, I cannot handle this, but you, oh God, are more than capable of handling it. It is an act of faith, and when we operate in this level of faith, it puts a demand on heaven to move on our behalf.

Worship Scriptures:

- Genesis 22:5
- Jeremiah 7:2 KJV
- John 4:20 KJV
- Psalm 105:3
- Psalm 29:2
- Psalm 95:6-7
- Zephaniah 3:9

When others see you take a stand and refuse to bow down, worship idols or things. God is honored and gloried.

- Daniel 3:28-29: Nebuchadnezzar answered and said, "Blessed be the God of Shadrach, Meshach, and Abednego, who has sent his angel and delivered his servants, who trusted in him, and set aside[a] the king's command, and yielded up their bodies rather than serve and worship any god except their own God. Therefore I make a decree: Any people, nation, or language that speaks anything against the God of Shadrach, Meshach, and Abednego shall be torn limb from limb, and their houses laid in ruins, for there is no other god who is able to rescue in this way."

- **Acts 16:25-34 KJV**: And at midnight, Paul and Silas prayed, and sang praises unto God: and the prisoners heard them. And suddenly there was a great earthquake, so that the foundations of the prison were shaken: and immediately all the doors were opened, and every one's bands were loosed. And the keeper of the prison awaking out of his sleep, and seeing the prison doors open, he drew out his sword, and would have killed himself, supposing that the prisoners had been fled. But Paul cried with a loud voice, saying, Do thyself no harm: for we are all here. Then he called for a light, and sprang in, and came trembling, and fell down before Paul and Silas, And brought them out, and said, Sirs, what must I do to be saved? And they said, Believe on the Lord Jesus Christ, and thou shalt be saved, and thy house. And they spake unto him the word of the Lord, and to all that were in his house. And he took them the same hour of the night, and washed their stripes; and was baptized, he and all his, straightway. And when he had brought them into his house, he set meat before them, and rejoiced, believing in God with all his house.

The enemy knows the power that we have when we begin to worship in prayer, and so he goes to great lengths to get us to worship other gods or to walk in idolatry. Jesus understood that God is the only person who should be worshiped, and he openly rebuked the enemy when he tried to deceive him concerning worship.

All these things I will give you if You fall down and worship me. Then Jesus said to him, Get away from here, Satan! For it is written, You shall worship the Lord your God, and Him only shall you serve.
Matthew 4:9-10

As great a weapon as worship is, God hates idolatry. Throughout the entire Bible, we see how strongly God feels against idolatry. There are consequences for those who worship other gods instead of the only true and living God. Jeremiah 16:11 states, *"Then you shall say to them: Because your fathers have forsaken Me, says the Lord, and have walked after other gods and have served them and have worshiped them, but have forsaken Me and have not kept my law."* Idol worship hinders our communication with God. To utilize worship as an effective weapon in prayer, it's critical to worship the only true and living God!

As I conclude this chapter, I want to remind you that your weapons are useless unless you properly use them. Every person in the military has weapons that they use in the time of the battle. They are always in uniform and dressed for the battle, even in a time of peace. Never lay your weapons down. You don't want them to become ineffective by not using them. There will be seasons where you have to praise while hurting. Worship while healing. Keep God at the center of all you do and stay in his word. This will keep you grounded.

ASSIGNMENT

How will you use these weapons of God in your prayer life?

_____

_____

_____

Are there any weapons we've discussed that you haven't put into use?

_____

_____

_____

How can you execute them?

_____

_____

_____

CHAPTER KEYS

1. Spiritual weapons are only effective when they are used.

2. Praise keeps you in a place of gratitude.

3. God has already given you authority over the adversary/Satan. Use God's word to defeat the enemy of your soul.

4. Everyone and everything can praise God. True worship can only come from those who worship God in spirit and in truth.

5. Apply the Word of God to every situation, and you will get effective results.

6. Declare the Word of God by speaking, decreeing, and declaring what you want to see, and it will manifest as long as it is in the will of God.

CHAPTER SEVEN

THE ARMOR OF GOD: DRESSING PROPERLY FOR PRAYER

As I write this chapter, it is 4:15 a.m. on a Friday morning. I have to work today. I woke up around 3:00 a.m. My bible study group and I have been reading the book of Ephesians again this week. As I read Ephesians 6:13 (KJV), I notice Paul's instructions. Wherefore *take* unto you the whole armour of God, that you will be able to withstand in the day of evil. He mentions the word "*take*." Most of us are used to using the word *take*. For example, "Can you take me to the store?" or "Will you have time today to take me _____?" In these instances, we are making a request of some sort and getting what we need to accomplish done with others' assistance.

Paul empowers us, admonishes us, and sends a friendly reminder that we need to put on every piece of armor and be dressed for the battle. He describes this armor and gives us a picture of how the Roman soldiers dressed for day-to-day battle or combat. When he wrote this passage, it was from a familiar place. He spent a lot of time writing in jail. So, he was able to grasp this very concept from the confinements of his cell. Bound and chained to stay confined to a particular place with soldiers marching all around.

Here Paul commissions us to take or put on our armor. These items must be picked up and put on. Just as we get dressed daily for work, morning workouts, church, errands, we have to dress for the battle. Your Armor is not going to just get up and place itself on you. Your armor does not have hands or feet. You have to be intentional. Each piece is equally as important as the next. Together they make an unstoppable garment of prayer. Have you ever met anyone in law enforcement, the military, a firefighter, bus driver, or crossing guard while on duty? Notice that they all have one thing in common. All of them have on a uniform—a shirt, a pair of pants, a belt, shoes, holsters, etc. None of them show up for work undressed.

What does it mean to *take* or *put on* something? Take (verb) means to "lay hold of something with one's hands; to reach hold of; remove someone or something from a particular place." "Put (verb) move to or place in a particular position; bring into a particular state or condition." (Oxfords Dictionary).

Read the following verses and draw a circle each time Paul mentions the word *take* or ***put on***.

Ephesians 6:10-18

10 A final word: Be strong in the Lord and in his mighty power.
11 Put on all of God's armor so that you will be able to stand firm against all strategies of the devil.
12 For we are not fighting against flesh-and-blood enemies, but against evil rulers and authorities of the unseen world, against mighty powers in this dark world, and against evil spirits in the heavenly places.

13 Therefore, put on every piece of God's armor so you will be able to resist the enemy in the time of evil. Then after the battle, you will still be standing firm.

14 Stand your ground, putting on the belt of truth and the body armor of God's righteousness.

15 For shoes, put on the peace that comes from the Good News so that you will be fully prepared.

16 In addition to all of these, hold up the shield of faith to stop the fiery arrows of the devil.

17 Put on salvation as your helmet, and take the sword of the Spirit, which is the word of God.

18 Pray in the Spirit at all times and on every occasion. Stay alert and be persistent in your prayers for all believers everywhere.

As we prepare to go before the Lord in prayer, we must remember that we do not go into the presence of the Lord in any kind of way. His very presence commands our respect, reverence, our focus, and our appearance. Our armor demonstrates that we are ready to both hear from God and to war on his behalf. After all, he is our commander in chief. His soldiers must properly dress for battle.

Paul tells us to put on "the whole" armor of God so that you will be able to stand in the day of adversity. Stand in the day of battle; to overcome the evil one. He says, put on the belt of truth, righteousness, peace, and salvation. What does it really mean to put on something? If a person has to tell you to put something on, they are giving you a friendly reminder of what is missing or what you will need for where you are going. In our day-to-day walk, we are faced with many things. There will be many opportunities to make decisions that will have long-term effects.

When we put on truth, we're making a statement that we
will use the Word of God, not what man nor the enemy said.
When we are praying, we must be in a position to hear from
God and drown out the background noise of our minds and
thoughts. Looking back at some of the choices we've all made,
we can honestly admit that our armor at times has been rusty, dusty, or not used
properly. This is why we have to **put on truth,** or our minds wander all over the
place at times. There are times when we are being hit from every side. Here's
where we have to deal with the reality of a matter. I can choose to believe what
is true, accept it for what it is, operate in it, or let it operate me. Truth is the
quality or state of being true. (Oxford Dictionary) Ask yourself, what does God's
word say about this? What is God saying about this? Have I been in this place
before, and what was the outcome?

Some battles we don't get to pick. However, we do get to play a key
component in the outcome. Satan is our enemy. He does not want you to operate
in truth. After all, it is the truth that makes us free and keeps us free. Truth is
what protects us, keeps us grounded, and gives us the right perspective.
Deception, not the truth, is what leads to harm. The Word of God says that our
righteousness is as filthy rags before the Lord. Yet Paul says to **put on
righteousness**. Here is where we have to take a moment
to truly identify how we are operating in the spirit. Those
who operate in the spirit and who live spirit-led lives will not
fulfill the lust of the flesh. It is our God-given right as his
children through the shed blood of Jesus Christ and through

his redemptive power that we are able to put on the full armor of God. Don't take this lightly. Accepting Jesus' sacrifice puts each of us in right standing with God. We have to keep our hearts and minds clean.

As defined by the Student Bible Dictionary, *righteousness* is defined as "right or just, right with God. A person is made right only through God in Christ." Any person who is not in right standing with God will not be allowed to enter into his presence. When praying, it is very important to confess or repent of your sins so you will encounter his presence. There will be times when you're praying, and the enemy of your soul will try to condemn you. His goal is to make you feel unworthy. This is when you take the time to address your righteousness in Christ Jesus and remind him that there is no condemnation for those who are in Christ Jesus (Romans 8:1 NLT).

David asked the Lord to create a clean heart in him and renew in him a right spirit. David pleaded with the Lord, "please do not take your spirit from me but restore unto me the joy of your salvation." All of us have had heart issues. These issues can be deeply rooted in past hurts, failures, disappointment, or even self-inflicted. Our hearts can become tainted from the evil we see at work all around us. We're affected by what we watch on TV, listen to via media, or simply by what we witness in our day-to-day lives.

Put on the helmet of salvation to guide you from the evilness of this world. It protects you from being misinformed by the enemy himself. There is a war going on at this very moment concerning your mind. This war is designed to keep you filled with distractions, especially when praying. Protect your mind when praying. God wants to speak to you, and you must be in a position to hear from him. Scriptures say that we should let our mind be like the mind of Christ Jesus. If your mind isn't in Christ Jesus, what is it in? We must equip our minds with the truth of God's word. The world we live in does not provide the right

Helmet Of Salvation

knowledge. Some of us get caught up in the wrong way of thinking before we're in Christ due to the things we were taught, learned, introduced to, false teaching, or our environments. I grew up living and visiting Louisiana. We would visit the French Quarters, and you could see women swinging in and out of windows in the saloons, half-dressed, or not dressed at all. There were tables set up with palm readers who wanted so badly to tell you of your future and warn you of the evil spirits that so desired to have you. There was witchcraft practiced on every side of the street and in unimaginable places. I became very fearful of certain environments, including the church. When I went to the beauty shop or hairdresser, I rarely let anyone cut my hair, and if I did, I would kindly ask for the broom and sweep my hair up or asked them to put my hair in an envelope and give it back to me because I didn't want anyone to put *roots* on me by keeping my hair. After I came to accept and know Christ, I realized that all of this was twisted thinking and wrong knowledge.

If you ever read the book of Genesis, you know all too well that the Egyptians' fake seers, soothsayers, and magicians duplicated every demonstration Moses did at the command of God. The only difference is their demonstration was counterfeit and fueled by Satan. They were creating illusions of what appeared to be real. The Lord freed me from all of this one day. Some of the ladies I attended church with had very nicely kept hair. I asked a few of them who did their hair, and amazingly, they all had the same stylist. I asked who she was, and I was introduced to her. She agreed to do my hair, and I never looked back. I never felt as if I paid her enough for her services. I came to her salon broken, yet God used her to heal my mind, change my thought process, and my heart. To this day, we are very close, and I never asked her for my hair.

Put on peace. God's name means peace, Jehovah Shalom. When we are putting on peace, we are actually putting on God. We are taking on the very nature of God. Peace doesn't always mean that we will live absent from conflict or war. It just means we choose to take the position that we will not let it create a disturbance in us, especially while praying. Have you ever went to work and said, I've got to get this done today, and I can't have anyone disturbing me, or I've got certain tasks that are due by a certain time, and everything that could happen just took over, one obstacle after the next, after the next, etc. Your children, spouse, or friends all have an emergency... that really could wait. That boss who doesn't plan so well now wants their lack of planning to infringe on your priorities. I know it makes you want to scream. There have been times when I did scream for lack of better words. This is where you need to put on peace.

Scripture teaches us that you have to dust your feet and walk away if you enter a place and you sense that you are not welcome. Here's where we are commanded to take our peace and take the nearest exit. Our greatest commission is to take the gospel into the world. I believe our elder disciples had it much harder than we do. Unlike us, they had to travel by foot on dusty roads to minister the gospel. Often, they had to stay in the homes of other believers who would take them in. Paul often wrote letters just to get his message to the people. Yet, we can hop on social media and reach the world in a matter of seconds. We can travel by car, bus, or private jet, yet we are not as effective.

How are you spreading this gospel? Are we living in a way that this gospel can go forth in peace and be effective? Do you have the proper shoes on? The Roman soldiers wore sandals with straps that covered their entire calf and most of their legs. These sandals had spikes under the soles of the shoe to keep their feet from slipping. This design detail was added so they could keep their grip in battle, running, or walking in unknown territories. Their sandals were an important part of the soldier's arsenal. They could use the spikes on the shoes to defend themselves. If their opponent came up from behind them, all they had to do was kick them and inflect a womb immediately, causing damage.

Shoes were used as a protective covering. Even professional athletes have to wear certain shoes to protect their feet. Boxers don't show up to a match in heels. Football players, soccer players, and both softball and baseball players wear cleats. How else can they stand firm? Can you imagine a football player trying to kick a field goal in heels? Add this to rainy days or snow on the field. Sounds like a recipe for a great disaster. Professional dancers and gymnasts even wear certain shoes as protective gear for their feet. Please check your shoes before you leave home today. Psalm 91 promises us that we will walk on serpents and tread upon lions, scorpions, etc. We can't accomplish this barefooted. Use your shoes in prayer to step on the head of every enemy. Every place you encounter is a battleground. Go and put on your shoes.

Take up the shield of faith. Certain careers or industries require shields to protect themselves. Doctors and dentists wear shields over their faces when performing certain medical procedures. Military and law enforcement agents wear shields when preparing for battle or for certain assignments. They wear protective gear under their shirts to protect the chest, heart, and upper body parts as well. The Roman soldiers would carry shields at all times. In the event of an attack from the enemy, they would form circles and quickly connect their shields to protect themselves from the flaming arrows that were being launched at them. The shield covers the entire formation, and not a single person was left uncovered. We must do the same.

Shield Of Faith

Sword of The Spirit

Take the Sword of the Spirit, which is the Word of God. Most of us know that a sword is a sharp object used to cut, wound, or destroy its opponent when used correctly. Every sword has a very sharp point at the end of it. This is what causes objects to be pierced. Bring the Word of God to pray with you by any means necessary. The sword of the spirit is the Word of God. The Word of God teaches us that angels harken to the voice of God and through his word. Applying the Word of God in prayer ensures that you do not pray outside of the will of God. Praying the Word of God keeps you grounded. The sword, coupled with the word, cancels the enemy's plot, making his tactic ineffective. In order words, this is how we effectively assassinate the enemy on the battleground. Seek the Word of God for scripture reference for what you face.

Write them out, pray them out loud, and constantly apply them to the situation. This guarantees significant results.

ASSIGNMENT

What are some of the flaming darts or arrows the enemy has launched or is currently launching at you? _____

_____

_____

Are you prepared to combat and dressed for the battle? _____

_____

_____

What have you done or are in the process of doing to ensure your armor is in full use? _____

_____

_____

In verse 18, Paul tells us to pray in the spirit at all times and on every occasion. Stay alert and be persistent in your prayers for all believers everywhere. When we accepted Jesus Christ as our Lord and Savior, the Holy Spirit of God manifested itself inside of us. He guides us in every area of our lives. This is different from praying in the spirit. Romans 8:26 (NASB) reads as follows; the Holy Spirit helps us in our weakness. For example, we don't know what God wants us to pray for. But the Holy Spirit prays for us with groaning that cannot be expressed in words. Praying in the spirit or *praying in tongues* are perfect prayers. Direct communication that keeps you connected to the Father. As a matter of fact, scripture teaches us that there were believers who have not received the Holy Spirit since they believed. They were asked, "Have you received the Spirit since you believed?" Their response was we haven't heard of this Spirit. So, my question to you today is, have you been filled with the Holy Spirit, and have you received the gift of speaking in tongues since you believed? If you haven't, ask God to fill you with this free gift that only comes from him.

Start by reading the book of John, Psalms, or the book of Acts so that you can develop an understanding. Search the scriptures on speaking in tongues, meditate on them. Get in a quiet place and wait on the Lord. Start by worshipping the Lord, and have some instrumental worship music in the background. Create a place for God to meet you and wait on Him. Over some time, you will find that God will already be there. He wants to spend time with you.

If you attend a spirit-filled church, go kneel at the altar; seek God's face; ask God to reveal himself to you. You will experience God in a new way. It's ok to ask one of the church elders to assist you in this area as well. Study *tarrying*, this is the way the older saints were filled. The younger generation may say it does not take all of this, but I believe if you want something bad enough, you will sacrifice and pay the price.

We must pray for believers everywhere. In every nation, not just the ones you know, like, or prefer. We have to cover each other and our families in prayer. We never know what others are going through. In certain countries, believers are still being killed and hiding to keep from being persecuted. Remember, our struggle isn't against flesh and blood, but against the evil one. The battle is still going on in heavenly places. Start by covering your city, state, and local communities. Over a period of time, add other states, countries, etc. It takes time to build to this. It is not going to happen overnight, but you will make progress over time.

Prayer

Heavenly Father, as I put on the full armor of God today. I asked that you would equip me for what lies ahead. Teach me the truth of your word so that I will not be overtaken by the wiles and schemes of the devil. I cancel every counterfeit agent of the evil one that is at work in dark places. I put on the belt of truth this morning, the truth of your word, and the truth of who you say that I am so that I will not be overtaken by the power of the enemy.

My prayer is that you would create a clean heart in me, renew in me a right spirit, and cleanse my heart from all of its evil desires. Cleanse me from sinful fleshly desires. Forgive me for putting filthy and worthless things before my eye gates, ear gates, or things that have tried to attach themselves to me from the seeds of others. Let my mind be in Christ Jesus so that I can receive peace this day. I cancel the plot of the evil one who would attempt to control my mind by any means. I plead the blood of Jesus over my mind, heart, and every part of my life.

I put on shoes of peace today so that I may walk in love wherever I go and spread your love and message as I go about my day. Forgive me for the days I did not walk in a matter worthy of the calling you have assigned over my life. I choose peace today and when it is hard, shield me.

I take the shield of faith and tear down every assignment of the enemy this day. Father, dispatch the angels that you have assigned over my life to guard and protect me each day of my life so that I will complete the assignment you have for my life. In Jesus' name, amen!

CHAPTER KEYS

1. The Holy Spirit prays for us with groaning that cannot be expressed in words. He is praying because we do not know what to pray.

2. Stand in the day of adversity and in the time of battle by putting on the full armor of God.

3. We are all filled with the Holy Spirit once we accept Christ; however, we must activate the gift of speaking in tongues.

4. The Holy Spirit guides us in prayer and in our day-to-day activities.

CHAPTER EIGHT
WHY DO WE KEEP PRAYING?

We have to be persistent and keep praying to tear down the enemy's demonic attacks and usher in God's perfect will on earth. No matter what is going on in life, we have to keep praying! 1 Thessalonians 5:16-18 of the New Living Translation bible reads as follows, "Always be joyful. Never stop praying. Be thankful in all circumstances, for this is God's will for you who belong to Christ Jesus." Verse 17 clearly, states never stop praying. I know life has a way of knocking you down, creating its own assignment for your life, and in the back of your mind, you're thinking, "Did I sign up for all of this?"

While I was working on my bachelor's degree, I came to a crossroads. I wondered if it was really worth all of this. I spent several years previously working on my associate degree, graduated from a two-year college, and I felt this was enough. There were days I was tired, adjusting to a new way of life, and had recently moved to another state. The schools I previously attended were on a semester system, whereas this college was on a quarter system. It seemed like every time I looked up, something was due, and a new quarter was starting. One day, something in me said, do not give up. I had many conversations with the Lord, and for some reason, he would not allow me to quit.

Each semester I would pray the same prayer. Lord, just help me to pass this class. Once I got to what looked like the finished line, I could not graduate as planned. Every student was given a test that they had to take and pass to receive their degree. I took this test numerous times but did not pass it. Every time I said if I do not pass this exam, I am not taking it again. I prayed before each exam and got the same result and would have to retake the exam. Finally, one night while sitting in a small group meeting, the leader of the group said, "Erica, I see you coming up the hill, like at the end of the movie Rocky and you have on your boxing gloves, and you're fighting. The next morning, I went to take the exam, and I felt more confident than ever before. Amazingly this time, I imaged a bell going off in my mind, I saw myself in the boxing ring, and before I knew it, the exam was over. I left class so excited and thanking God. This time when those results came in the mail, I passed. Thank you, Jesus!

Keep praying. You may not understand why. Just know that this could be for a ministry, a child, a business, healing for a loved one, a promotion, a trip, or a vehicle. Keep praying, no matter what. Once I passed that exam, I knew I had crazy faith. So many times, we give up on the verge of the answer. Being consistent in prayer develops your faith, keeps the focus on God and not self, and what you can't accomplish on your own. It builds your testimony. We overcome the evil one and everything we face by the blood of the Lamb and the word of our testimony. Once my daughter went to college, I later understood that if I did not break the cycle of women not finishing school in my family, she would have had the same struggle. Decide today that you are going to finish what you start so that cycles can be broken.

The more we pray, the more we build our relationship with God. It keeps the lines of communications open. Could you imagine dating someone and never hearing from him or her? In your mind, you're thinking, do we really have a relationship. On the other hand, think about the person that only contacts you when they need or want something. Eventually, you would just move on.

When we pray, we not only keep the lines of communication open for us to talk to God, but he also speaks to us. He gives us instructions for our lives and insight into what his plans are for our lives. He showers us with His unfailing love. We discern his voice better and sense his presence. I believe that if I gave up and did not show up for the exam, my prayer would have never been answered. The enemy of my mind would still be saying, "If you took the exam, you might have passed it." This victory would have been a permanent defeat by default. Keep praying until you get your answer. Only God can release you from a prayer assignment.

Constant praying helps you to develop a higher level of expectation, self-worth, and confidence. By doing this, you put a demand on both God and heaven as your faith grows. In other words, be excited and have a level of expectancy about the things you believe God for in prayer. Make a conscious decision that you are going to pray no matter what. Be intentional, even if you need to find a prayer partner who is willing to pray with you for a certain period to make this happen. The scripture says that God sought for someone to pray, and he could not find anyone. Be intentional and pray with a purpose.

As you go through life, you will encounter situations that you do not know how to handle. Call on the Lord. Simply ask the Father in prayer to assist you. Make your request known. You do not have to beat around the bush with God. He already knows what we need. This is considered "making supplication."

- **John 4:2**

  You desire but do not have, so you kill. You covet, but you cannot get what you want, so you quarrel and fight. You do not have because you do not ask God.

- **Philippians 4: 6-7**

  Do not be anxious about anything, but in every situation, by prayer and petition, with thanksgiving, present your requests to God. And the peace of God, which transcends all understanding, will guard your hearts and your minds in Christ Jesus.

EXERCISE

What areas in your life have you been struggling with? _____

_____

_____

Can you call on the name of the Lord for help? _____

_____

_____

FURTHER STUDY

- 1 Thessalonians 5:16-18
- James 5:17b
- Jeremiah 33:3
- Mark 11:24
- Matthew 7:8
- Psalm 145:18
- Psalm 18:6

When God Does Not Answer the Way, I Expect

Have you ever wanted something so bad until you just knew God was going to give it to you just the way you wanted it? You prayed, affirmed it with the Word of God, decreed and declared it, called your friends, family, prayer partners, everyone stood in agreement, and God gives you a big fat NO. You then sit there in awe like God, are you serious. Did this happen? You began to question yourself and God. Then you hear the famous words "it's not time." I can remember when I wanted to work for this company so bad until I just knew God was going to open the door. I had all of the right contacts and great relationships with the staff. I completed the job application, interviewed for the position, discussed salary, a schedule, and picked out the workspace only for God to close the door. Do you know how disappointed I was? When you get this far in the process, and the door closes. Why God?

At that point, I took a different path. God always has a better plan for our lives. Jeremiah 29:11 says that God knows the plans he has for us. God's plans are good for us, and they protect us even when we do not understand them. Think about that relationship you wanted, and it ended or never grew into what you expected. As time passed, you began to praise God for some of the doors closing. Let's examine and study Paul's, David's, and Jesus' response to God's perfect NO.

Paul

In 2 Corinthians 12:1-10, Paul is ministering to the people, and he is giving them an account of an experience, a vision he had when God allowed him to be caught up in the third heaven and the result of the vision. Paul first explains to the people that while he was having the vision, he did not know whether he was in the body or out of the body, but he does know that the experience happened. He remembers that this encounter happened at least fourteen years ago. Now, this must have been some encounter that he is still talking about it fourteen years later. Paul also acknowledges that God is the only one who truly knows if he was in or out of his body. Some people refer to these moments as out-of-body experiences but not in a godly way. He takes the time to tell the audience that he was in paradise and overheard conversations of such great magnitude that no human would repeat them. Have you ever witnessed anything like this? God would have had to put a serious gate over my mouth to keep me from telling what I saw. I would have wanted everyone to know what I experienced. He admits that sharing this exciting experience would not do any good to discuss in one of the verses. He declares that I will not boast about what I saw, but I am willing to discuss my weaknesses.

In verse seven, Paul stated that he received a thorn in his side from a messenger of Satan. This messenger tormented him day after day, repeatedly. It got to the point that Paul began to cry out and beg the Lord on three different occasions to remove it. Paul alleges that this was placed there to keep him humble. Now, why would God allow this to happen? After watching Joyce Meyers one day, she addressed the passage by stating that God would always keep us in a place where we have to depend on him. God could have removed this thorn the very moment he pleaded with him. Instead of removing the thorn, God responds by saying, "My grace is all you need. My power works best in weakness." From that moment, Paul never asked God to remove that thorn again. He moved on and declared the following words, " That's why I take pleasure in my weaknesses, and in the insults, hardships, persecutions, and troubles that I suffer for Christ. For when I am weak, then I am strong."

REFLECTION QUESTIONS

Who afflicted Paul and why was he afflicted?_____

_____

_____

How many times did Paul plead to God? _____

_____

_____

Why do you believe God did not remove this thorn from Paul's side?_____

_____

_____

When was the last time you made a petition or made a request of God and he did not answer the way you thought? _____

_____

_____

What was God's response and how did you receive or respond to it?_____

_____

_____

Looking back, do you count it as a blessing, or are you still disappointed?

_____

_____

_____

Go back to verse nine and write it out in the space provided. Do you really believe this? _____

_____

_____

David

As we review the life of David before he became king, we know that in the natural eye, most did not think very much of David in the beginning. David was born outside of marriage and most likely known to his family as the smelly shepherd boy from childhood to adulthood. God called the prophet Samuel to stop by the home of a man named Jesse one day. Jesse was the father of David. As the prophet spoke with his dad, he revealed to him the nature of his visit. God sent him to the home of Jesse to anoint his next king. The person who would replace King Saul. According to the scriptures, Jesse called in all of his sons except David. Finally, the prophet asked if he had another one. His dad says (paraphrasing), oh yeah, my son David. Therefore, he sends for David. When he arrived, smelling like the great outdoors with a touch of animal sent, the prophet says here he is. Our next king just entered the house. The Bible says that the prophet Samuel anoints him as king while the current king is still in office.

Before David took his royal position, we all know that he was not only a shepherd, but he played the harp for King Saul when the evil spirits would come upon him. He defeated the great giant Goliath and was a natural-born warrior. I present this to point out that David still had heart issues, just as we all do.

Take some time to read 2 Samuel 11 and 12 to get an understanding of why God did not answer David's prayer. In chapter 12, we learn that King David is not at war with his men as he should have been. He looks outside of his bedroom window and notices the beautiful silhouette of Bathsheba. Bathsheba is the wife of one of his soldiers named Uriah. David chose to call this woman over and defile her bed and his by becoming intimately involved with her. Later he finds out that she is with child. David has a problem on his hands. He has to clean this mess he made up. He calls for Uriah and tries to persuade him to have sexual relations with his wife while he is off duty. Uriah is so devoted to serving David until he does not go home as instructed. After several days, David realizes that Uriah is not going home and sleep with his wife. David gives Uriah a note and instructs him to give it to his captain. Uriah, unlike me, did not read this note. I would have held the note up to the light just to see if I could see what the note said. He did not want to seem distrustful by the king or his commander. David had Uriah put in the heat of the battle, and he dies.

David takes Bathsheba as his wife and moves her into his palace. They both know that David is the father of this child. After some time, God sends the prophet Nathan to see King David. The prophet Nathan tells David a story of a man who only has one lamb, and the rich man who had plenty took it. He even explained how much the man loved the lamb and took care of the lamb. David became so enraged until he said a man who commits such a crime deserves to pay four times what he stole and even death. Then Nathan springs it on him and says, David, you are the man. The word says that David then falls to the ground and repents. The prophet tells him that God has forgiven him, but this forgiveness still came with a punishment. God required his son. The son of him and Bathsheba.

Once David counted the cost of his sins and what God was requiring, he fasted. The word says that none of his servants could get him to eat. David fasted for seven days, pleading with the Lord to spare this baby's life. On day seven, the baby dies, and his servants were afraid to tell him that the child died. David looks out and sees that his servants are talking, and he simply asked, "Is the child dead?" They replied, yes. Once he heard the news, David gets up, shakes himself off, takes a bath, put on some lotion, changes his clothes, and goes to the tabernacle and worship the Lord. Once he returned home, he ate and moved on.

His servants were in awe. They could not believe that he fasted while the child was sick and ate when he died.

In closing, David took the position that there is nothing he humanly could do at this point. It is time to move on. I cannot bring him back. I have accepted what God has done. The Bible says that David was intimate with Bathsheba, and she conceived again. This time, this child was of the Lord, and they named him Solomon. Solomon would one day sit on the throne after King David. God's no can lead to the biggest blessing of your life.

Jesus

We all know that Jesus knew exactly who he was and clearly understood that he was born to die. In fact, he reminded God that he was returning to the position he had before this assignment. He was planning his great return; To finally sit in his rightful place.

Taking some time to review Mark 14 and 15, notice that Jesus, while filled with anguish, took James, John, and Peter with him one night to pray. As Jesus goes to pray, alone, he makes one request of them "sit here while I go and pray." Jesus was not the least bit surprised that he would find them asleep when he returned. He informs them of his current condition. His soul filled with grief unto the point of death. Scripture confirms that Jesus asks the Father to take his bitter cup from him. He knew God was well capable of making anything possible. Even as he prays to God, he says, "I know with you all things are possible." He even tells God that he wanted God's will over his. How many of us can truly say that we are ok with God's will over ours? Honestly speaking, I still battle with this. Having to know every deal, the outcome, overthinking the process, etc.

As Jesus returns, the three of them are still asleep. This time he addresses Peter. I am sure he had a firm tone. He says Peter, are you sleep? Could you not watch and pray? Listen, Peter, I need you to watch and pray. You are headed to a road called temptation, and you are not going to be ready for what is ahead. His spirit is willing, but his flesh is weak. In other words, strengthen yourself in prayer so that the trials of life do not overcome you. Evil is waiting to overtake you at any given moment. You must feed your spirit by studying God's Holy Word. What you have inside of you is not quite strong enough. Jesus makes three trips to find them in the same posture asleep. I believe this place in scriptures informs us that there will be times in your life well, you will have to pray, even if you have to pray all by yourself. I know that we all have family, friends, or acquaintances that we can call on when we need prayer, but the truth of the matter is sometimes they just cannot help. Finally, Jesus just lets them sleep. They could not stay awake and did not know how to pray.

Remember that both God and Jesus are one. In this case, Jesus has to stand-alone. God is not going to take his cup. Jesus is going to have to complete this assignment while God sits backs and watches. God's plan was that man be reconciled to him and lead to the salvation of many. This includes both you and me, our families, friends, and enemies. God is not willing that any of us perish but come to salvation. Before the foundation of this world, God's plan was that we might be saved, spared from the gates of hell and that we might have eternal life with him. God knew that if he took that cup, many would remain sinners.

In closing, remember that God does not always answer the way we expect, but his answer is always perfect. I encourage you to take some time and reflect on this. Jot out your thoughts. Further study the scriptures. Consult God on his response to your situation.

 CHAPTER KEYS

1. God intended that man be reconciled to him. Had God intervened on Jesus' behalf, man would not have been redeemed to God. We would still need a redeemer.
2. We must remain steadfast in prayer to overcome the evil that lies ahead.
3. There will be times when you will need to pray alone, and it will appear that God is not with you. Continue to pray and watch God's plan manifest in your life just as it did when Jesus was faced with praying alone—yes, praying alone while his disciples slept.

CHAPTER NINE

PRAYER WARRIORS OF THE BIBLE

Wikipedia states that a prayer warrior "is a term used by many evangelicals and other Christians to refer to anyone who is committed to praying for others. Within the context of Dominion theology, prayer warriors see themselves as engaged in spiritual warfare against satanic forces." (Wikipedia) Ephesians 6:12 reminds us that we do not wrestle nor fight against flesh (people) and blood (natural things) but against evil, dark demonic places in heavenly places. In other words, there are battles and wars that are going on in the heavenly realms that we know nothing about, yet we are actively participating in them.

God used ordinary people in his Word to accomplish His will on the earth. God assigns each warrior to his or her assigned city, state, region, or territory. Abraham prayed to God concerning Sodom and Gomorrah (Genesis 18:16-33).

While his prayers did not spare that city from God's wrath, it spared Lot and his daughters. The principle we can learn from this is to pray for your family. God's original plan was to destroy the entire town, including the people, animals, businesses, etc. He did not plan to leave any stone unturned. Abraham's prayers changed the heart of God concerning his family, not the city. I believe Abraham prayed according to God's will.

Daniel prayed three times daily. All of his colleagues knew that he went home to pray at a certain time daily. His colleagues despised him so much until they wanted him dead. Yes, dead to the point that a few of them went to the king one day and convinced him to sign a decree that would ban anyone from petitioning any God or person other than him for thirty days, and if they did, they would be thrown into the lion's den, and this could not be revoked. The people Daniel worked with caused the king to make a decree to arrest Daniel and place him in a lion's den (Daniel 6:1-9). His colleagues knew that the only way to get rid of Daniel would have to be by his serving and praying to his God. Anyone who did not honor this decree would be found guilty of violating what the king set in place, which came with punishment. Once a king signs or makes a decree, it was irrevocable. Just as a judge sets an order in motion, it is set; it will not be overturned.

Once the king realized what happened and he could not change this decree. The king made this declaration over Daniel; "I pray that the God whom you serve saves you." The king was so upset that he did turn away his plate that night. In other words, the king fasted and mourned on his servant's behalf. This says a lot about the king's relationship with Daniel. While his colleagues were celebrating what looked like an end to Daniel, his God was answering the king's decree. God shut the mouths of the lions and spared Daniel's life. Unfortunately, those same lions ate his co-workers for breakfast. They got a three for one special. They fell into the pit or trap they set specifically for Daniel. Let this serve as a note to self that God will vindicate you and deal with your enemies. David prayed to God concerning his enemies and asked God for those who were after him to fall into their own traps, to spare his life, and they did!

Here are some more examples God answering the fervent prayers of his people:

- Hannah, according to 1 Samuel 1:12, was praying to the Lord while Eli watched. She never said a word. Only her lips moved; the prophet Eli was under the impression that she was drunk. God granted Hannah's request, she gave birth to the prophet Samuel, and none of his words fell to the ground. Hannah gave her first-born male son back to the Lord. As a result, the Lord opened up her womb, and she gave birth to other sons and daughters. Hannah pleaded with Lord. Isn't it amazing that you can get a prayer through without opening your mouth? Hannah was without a child, and in those days, women who were married were frowned upon if they could not bear children. Hannah's husband had another wife, who wasn't barren. She mocked Hannah tirelessly. Hannan knew in her heart that the only way she would give birth to a child was in the hands of GOD almighty. Hannah prayed, and she gave birth to the prophet Samuel and had other children (1 Samuel 1). The Word of God says that none of Samuel's words fell to the ground. Samuel anointed David to the Lord's work. God used Samuel to bring correction to the prophet Eli of what was to come of him and his children due to their disobedience to God and dishonoring his temple and the women of the land and his lack of correcting them.

- Elijah prayed, and it did not rain for years. As a matter of fact, it did not rain for three and a half years. He prayed again, it began to rain again, and the earth yielded her fruit. (1 Kings 17-18)

- Jesus prayed until it appeared that blood dropped from His head (Luke 22:44).

- God heard the cries (prayers) of the children of Israel, and He delivered them from their oppressors. (Exodus 3:7)

- When the believers prayed, Peter was freed from jail. The believers prayed with such fervency until Peter walking right into the midst of their prayer. (Act 12:5-17)

I believe that God will assign you to the places where you have lived and currently reside to cover in prayer. There have been times when God has given me instructions on praying for my hometown. I would intercede on the town's behalf. Some of those times, I had no idea as to what was going on or what was to come. God led me to pray. Other times, I will be home visiting, and the Lord would lead me to my old high school. I would drive over to the school and walk the track. While I walked, the Lord would have me praying for the staff, students, activities, parents, etc. On one occasion, I later spoke with a former classmate and told them that I had been over to the school, praying that day, and they stated to me that the day was peaceful. I praised God. To this day, I believe that I am to pray for that city even though I no longer reside there.

When you grow up in a place, you learn the language and customs of the land. God can use those things that you have learned to effectively teardown, pluck up, and root out things that have been looked over for years. Just as he can use you to bring change where no one knew there was a need. He can also cause you to aid the intercessors and prayer warriors of that particular place. God afforded me the opportunity to move away from my hometown, yet when I visit, I feel like I never left home. He has connected me to a body of believers who watch over my soul and pray for my family and me. They treat me like family, and I am never at a loss when I spend time with them in fellowship. He will bring you out so you can come back in.

ASSIGNMENT

Study the prayer lives of those who prayed in the Bible. Take notes of their lives and the results. Remember that praying will lead to victory and safety.

What can we learn from these lessons? _____

_____

_____

Are you a prayer warrior?_____

_____

_____

What areas of your life do you need some strengthen in concerning prayer?

_____

_____

_____

Make a list of those things and pray over them until you see the hand of God move._____

_____

_____

Earlier, as I was planning to write on biblical prayer warriors, I knew that Daniel would be one of the people whose lives would depict a true prayer warrior. When we first met Daniel, he is a slave in captivity, living in exile with a zeal for the Lord. Unlike most, he refused to obey the laws of the land that would defile the living God. Daniel developed a meaningful prayer life through steadfastness, obedience, and discipline. He prayed three times daily, had visions, and longed for his people to be freed from exile. Also, he fasted and mourned for at least three weeks for his people. I encourage each of you to do an intense study of the book of Daniel. This will help you to develop a concept of who he really is.

I no longer live in the city that I was born in. Yet, there are times when God will lead me to pray for both that city and state. On one occasion, God led me to have a prayer brunch to pray for that city. I invited those I knew had a true heart for that place and would assist in praying God's will. There will be times when you will have to carry this burden alone, just like Daniel. Let's take a moment to read Daniel 9:3-19. Here we discover that Daniel is once again praying for his people. We will take a moment to read this passage of scripture and then reflect on the importance of praying for the places you have lived. You will develop your personal prayer strategy for your God-given territories, county, city, state, regions, or jurisdiction. Just because you no longer reside there doesn't mean you're not called to pray for it.

ASSIGNMENT

Go back through the passage and underline everything that is speaking to you at this very moment. What stood out most?

How did Daniel approach God?_____

_____

_____

Daniel said that as he prayed, he made supplications before the Lord. What is the definition of supplication? _____

_____

_____

What were some of the things Daniel prayed about in this chapter?

_____

_____

_____

How did the people defile God?_____

_____

_____

What have you noticed about the places you have lived? It is amazing that once you live in a place, you notice a lot of things that just do not seem right.

_____

_____

_____

Do you believe that your prayers make a difference in this area? If so, what changes have you seen? _____

_____

_____

Do you believe our personal choices affect what God does in a place?_____

_____

_____

What did you learn from Daniels praying in the chapter? _____

_____

_____

_____

How can you implement what you have learned from Daniel's prayer life into your prayer strategies and make them more successful in this area?_____

_____

_____

PRAYER

Father God, in the name of Jesus, reveal to me the places and territories that you have given me to watch over and to cover in prayer. Reveal to me the strategy in which you have me to pray over these places. Show me the things that have held the people who live in those places back and what keeps them from coming forward. I need your guidance to establish the right principles and tools when I am praying. Please connect me to the people in these places who have divine insight so that I can more efficiently and effectively teardown every stronghold and demonic principalities that are working against the people of God and the people in this city. I release my family, myself, and those with whom I have relationships from the generational bondage that has been in our lives and pass down from generation to generation. Release us from the spirit of poverty and its mindset. I release us from the spirit of lack, insufficiency, or victimize mindset. I release us from false religions and doctrines that have held us back for generations. Give us wisdom in all of our doings. Whatever it is, Lord, I know that you will reveal it in time. Please show me what scriptures to pray so that I do not hit a miss and your Word does not go out or return void concerning this place. Please forgive my family and me of any sins that we committed while we lived in this place. Release us from any learned behaviors that have offended you and anyone else in our lives. I claim this region, place, and territory as yours. In Jesus' name, amen.

 CHAPTER KEYS

1. God assigns individuals to pray fervently for places in which they may or may not live.
2. Hannah knew that God was the only one who could deliver her out of barrenness.
3. Be mindful that people will set traps for you, but God will avenge you just as he did Daniel. Never conform to what is going around you that does not include God. You are his chosen vessel.

CHAPTER TEN
SPECIFIC PRAYERS
PETITIONS AND SUPPLICATION

As we start this chapter, we will discuss different types of prayers. Once again, they are in no particular order. However, no soldier goes into battle without being prepared. In fact, soldiers are trained and equipped for every situation they face. They have different ranks and assignments based on experience and position. Whether they are on or off duty, retired or active duty, they are dressed and ready for the occasion. They do not relinquish their authority or lose competence just because they're off duty or retired. We should live our lives in the same manner.

The Prayer of Faith

Is anyone among you sick (suffering)? I anyone cheerful? Let him sing psalms (praise and worship). Let him call for the elders of the church (pray), and let them pray over him, anointing him with oil in the name of the Lord. ***James 5:13-16***

The prayer of faith will save the one who is sick, and the Lord will raise him up. If he has committed sins, he is forgiven. Therefore, confess your sins to one another and pray for one another that you may be healed. The prayer of a righteous person has great power as it is working. The Prayer of Faith offers prayer for the healing of oneself and others. A different translation reads as follows: *Such a prayer offered in faith will heal the sick, and the Lord will make you well. And if you have committed any sins, you will be forgiven. Confess your sins to each other and pray for each other so that you may be healed. The earnest prayer of a righteous person has great power and produces wonderful results.*

There will be times when you will be contacted by friends, family, colleagues, past acquaintances, or associates to pray for others. Please take this seriously. Others' lives are in the balance, and only you and those persons' prayers will reach heaven on that person's situation. Pray as if this will be the last prayer you ever pray. Each person is a key component of what God is doing and to God's healing process. Some prayers will require intense labor, while others will seem effortless. Nevertheless, this is your assignment. Do you remember while the disciples were headed to the house of God to Worship and they encounter a young man begging on the street? They offered him healing.

When Jesus encountered the man lying at the pool, he asked him, "Do you want to be healed?" He had been in that state for quite some time. Jesus did not lay hands on him to recover. He simply said, "Get up, take up your mat." The man did just what Jesus commanded. Sometimes, we believe that if it is not *long* or *deep,* it cannot happen. Simply obey the command of the Lord and carry on. You are healed because Jesus said you are healed.

Faith is a belief not based on proof. In other words, you will not necessarily see, feel, or touch it. It does not take faith for anyone to sit in a chair. People rarely think that a chair will not hold them unless they have already fallen in that chair before, and it fell apart. Faith has substance. It is something of importance. Faith develops over time. If a person grows up in a negative environment, it will take time for their thinking to change because their belief system foundation is not secure.

I joined the concert band when I was in sixth grade. My music instructor chose my instrument. It took time for me to develop the necessary skills to both read music and develop the tone to play that instrument. My mom had enough faith in me until she purchased my instrument without knowing if I would learn to play one note. After I accomplished concert band, I went to Jr. High, and here came another level of growth. I joined the marching band. Now it was easy to join the band because I had the same instructor. I had the same instructor until I went to high school. The summer before high school, we had summer band practices and tryouts. At the end of summer practice, you had to audition, which was a completely new level. I am saying all of this to say the first step was to join the band, and over time, the skills and whatever else took time to learn. Faith is the same way, one day you are not sure, and after a few victories, you know that all things are possible because you have seen the hand of God move repeatedly. Faith and works are the key ingredients to developing your faith walk.

A few months ago, I became ill. I ate, completed a bible study session, and started feeling ill. As I stood in my restroom, I began to feel nauseous, and it appeared that I was going to faint. I remember saying to myself, "I need to sit down. I am about to faint." When I came to, I was lying on the floor. All I could remember saying was, "Did I pass out?" As I lay there, I began to beat on the wall, and no one heard me. I started beating on the floor in hopes that my daughter would hear me. I continued to beat on the wall and the floor. Eventually, my daughter heard me and came into the restroom, saying, "Mommy, are you calling me? What are you doing on the floor?" I said, "I passed out. Go and get your dad." I began to pray and quote this scripture repeatedly. "I will live and not die to declare the works of the Lord!" Lord, if I could only get to my bed, I know I will be alright. After several failed attempts to get me off the floor, I said call the ambulance, and I need to go to the ER. However, the fighter in me said, "No, you are not! You will live and not die to declare the works of the Lord." I asked the Lord to give me enough strength so I could push up, so my husband could pick me up off the floor. I felt as if I wore a ton of weight that day. The Lord did just that. Once he could pick me up, and we headed toward the bedroom, I kept repeating Lord, just give me the strength to get to the bed. I felt as if that bed was the hem of Jesus' garment. Once I made it to the bed, I knew I was ok.

God is moved by our faith, not just by our circumstances. The disciples of Jesus could not cast out a demon one day, and after watching Jesus cast the demon out, he was asked how come they could not do this. His response was that they didn't have enough faith. Some things are only accomplished by *faith and fasting*. If you had faith the size of a mustard seed, you could speak to that mountain, and it would move. In other words, your faith will determine the outcome of your circumstances.

There was a time in my life where I had very little faith. My faith was so small I would have disagreed with the Word of God that says God has given each of us a measure of faith. While sitting in a class at Church one night, one of the elders taught a class on faith. This was a required class for discipleship. The elder came from this very passage of scripture. While they were teaching, they did not realize that I had left the room for a moment. To keep from causing an interruption when I returned, I left a small crack in the door. The teacher concluded the text by stating if you had enough faith, you could speak to the door and command it to open. As they pointed to the door, I tapped the side of the door, and it opened. Not a single person knew I did that. At the end of class, I waited behind and told the teacher it was me that made that door open. To this day, I still remember the looks on the faces of the people in that room.

God granted Hannah's petition for a man seed because of her faith. It took faith for Mary to watch her son die for the sins of the world. She held on to the promise of her being a virgin giving birth to the Messiah. Simeon believed the prophecy that he would not die until he saw the Lord's Messiah. The nagging woman kept pledging with a judge who did fear God or man until her debt was canceled. The woman with the issue of blood received her healing because she had enough faith to believe that she would be whole if she could but reach the hem of Jesus' garment. The woman whose child needed healing and argues with Jesus until her child is healed, moved on his heart when she said even the dogs eat the crumbs that fall off the master's table.

Prayer for Healing

Father, in the name of Jesus, I lift up those who are ill today. Lord, you know what each person is facing in his or her health. Your Word says that the prayer offered in faith would bring healing to those who are sick. I cover them in the blood of Jesus. I decree that they are free from the spirit of infirmity. I speak to this infirmity; I command you to leave, dry up and dissolve in the name of Jesus. Every organ and tissue in their body functions the way you created it to function. The blood of Jesus is at work in your life, and by the stripes of Jesus, you are healed. Sickness and disease have no place in your life. You are a child of the Most High God. Jesus bore your infirmities, carried your sins away, and with his stripes, you are healed. Lord, I understand that some get sick for no apparent reason, but I know that you will get the glory out of this. Lord, if it is sin, I asked that you would free them from any sins that they may have committed that may have led to this illness. Every generational infirmity and iniquity is broke by the power of the Holy Ghost.

If you are facing any illness in your body. Make this declaration over your life (This prayer is a demonstration of how to pray for others in need of healing. Apply this to every diagnosis.):

I am free from every sickness and disease, both known and unknown to man. I release myself from the spirit of infirmity. Just because it runs in the family does not mean that it can touch me. I plead the blood of Jesus over my life and this diagnosis. Lord, remove every person out of my presence who is speaking against my life. I renounce anything that I may have said or done to bring this illness upon myself. Lord, when I am hungry, help me in my weakness to make the right choice.

Lord, I confess at times, I have not made the best choices in my life when it comes to eating and exercising. Please forgive me for every wrong choice. I free myself from bad eating habits and wrong choices that have led me down this path. Every word that does not line up to what you have spoken over my health, I send back to the enemy, and it will not manifest. In Jesus' name, amen.

The scripture says that one should call for the elders of the church and that they should pray for the sick. The Word also says that if any two touch and agree, it is done. There will be times when you will have to pray for the healing of others all alone. You will have to remove any obstacle that is a hindrance when you are praying. According to Acts 9:40, Peter put them all outside, and knelt and prayed; and turning to the body, he said, "Tabitha, arise." She opened her eyes, and when she saw Peter, she sat up.

A Prayer to Pray in Need of Supplication

Read Psalm 32:1-11NLT

Lord, I repent of my sins _____. I thank you for not remembering my sins once I confess them to you. Thank you for declaring me not guilty when we both know that I am guilty and deserve punishment. Thank you that Jesus took all of my sins and every punishment so that I would be declared innocent. I no longer walk in the shameful deeds of my past. I have been forgiven and redeemed. Forgive me for every time I did not repent of my sins and repeatedly sinned against you, your statutes, laws, and decrees. Thank you for keeping your hand upon me when you could have easily taken it off and allowed me to die in my mess. Lord, I asked that you continue to keep your hands upon me and never let me fall. On days when I feel defeated, sing over me with songs of deliverance and songs of victory that I may go forth in your purpose and that I might be strengthened for what lies ahead. Teach me and guide me so that I may live out your will and your purpose for my life. I understand that sin keeps me from you and your presence. I do not take this for granted. In Jesus' name, amen.

Different Types of Prayer

As we study the Word of God, we learn that there are many different types of prayers prayed throughout the Bible. From Genesis to Revelations, the people of God faced much opposition. Oppressed on every side, but the Lord delivered them out of all of their troubles. David asked the Lord to teach his hands to war and his fingers to fight. David was used to fighting bears with his bare hands while tending sheep. David later led vast armies of men to war. He lived a life of constant battle on and off the field. Victorious only by the hand of God who taught his hands to war and his fingers to fight. Let this be our example. Lord teach my hands to war and my fingers to fight.

ASSIGNMENT:

Study the following prayers. Beside each prayer, there is a definition of what it means as well as a scripture reference. Once you finish, write each of them out and put them to memory. Feel free to use this section to take notes or write them on index cards and post them throughout your home or in a journal to revisit later. Write out your thoughts, search for other scriptures to support what you have learned, and apply them to your life.

Prayer of Agreement

Agreement: harmony or accordance in opinion or feeling; a position or result of agreeing (Oxford Dictionary).

They all met together and were constantly united in prayer, along with Mary, the mother of Jesus, several other women, and the brothers of Jesus. ***Acts 1:14***

The Word of the Lord says that if any two of you touch and agree that it shall be done. It only takes two to settle on the agreement of marriage, be business partners, accountability partners, or have a child, etc. Understand any two can touch and agree for good or bad. Take a moment here and list some of the things or ideas you know you need someone to agree with you on. Write them out and ask God to lead you to the person who can assist you in accomplishing your goals. Make a list of things you no longer need or need to be reconstructed that will allow you to achieve your dreams, assignment, or goals.

Prayer of Request or Supplication

Request: an act of asking politely or formally for something.
Supplication: the action of asking or begging for something earnestly or humbly.

Even so, you have done well to share with me in my present difficulty. As you know, you Philippians were the only ones who gave me financial help when I first brought you the Good News and then traveled on from Macedonia. No other church did this. Even when I was in Thessalonica, you sent help more than once.

And this same God who takes care of me will supply all your needs from his glorious riches, which have been given to us in Christ Jesus Philippians 4:19. **Philippians 4:14-16,19**

At one time, I could not imagine this scripture being fulfilled in my life. I made some financial decisions that were not in my best interest. I maxed out every credit card I owned coupled with other debt. Top this off with very little income to work with and was a college student. As creditors began to call me, I became very frustrated. I had more month left than money at times. I learned to trust God to supply every need I had. Often, I felt like how can I ask God to get me out of something he never orchestrated?

Going through this process, I learned several things about God being the source of provision. God who gives (supplies) every seed to the one who sows. God provided manna to the Israelites daily while traveling through a place of uncertainty. Jesus gave the disciples instructions to go back and cast their nets while fishing and for the money to pay the tax collector. It is not until we learn to trust God and his Word at face value that we comprehend that he has us covered in every aspect of our lives. The same God that gives seed to the sower causes the rain to fall on the seed and returns it with an unmeasured increase.

One day, I read a scripture that said, owe no man nothing but love. The Word of the Lord also teaches us to seek wise counsel. When I was engaged to my husband, we had a discussion about debt. His advice to me changed my whole perspective on debt. I remember him saying to me, pull your credit report, and pay off the smallest debt and move to the next one in that order. Also, see if they will allow you to make them an offer, get it in writing, and only work on that. I put this plan into action, and in a very short time, I had no debt. He also said not to speak negatively about this debt. You only have a few things that you need to clear up. What I learned in that season was to stick to the budget. If you cannot pay for it, you do not need it. Do not allow anyone to use your name for credit unless you are prepared to cover it. Before I make a major purchase, I seek God, and then I discuss it with my husband. I also have a dear friend who gives me wise counsel before I purchase anything. These strategies have helped me to help others. We must learn that the Power of Agreement starts with God and is confirmed by man.

The Lord already knows what you need before you ask. Scripture teaches us that God already knows what we need before we ask him. Let's agree to come to a place where we live our lives in a way that we can be a blessing to others, yet please God. Supplication does not just apply to what you need but to the needs of others as well. Neither is it just for monetary, but it's for healing, deliverance, breakthrough, and much more. Whatever you need, God will and can supply it. Take a moment and make a list of the things that you and those you know have unmet needs, and pray this prayer on your behalf and theirs. Once you pray, this prayer began to thank God that it is already supplied. God hears us the first time we pray.

I am a testament to God's provision and his goodness. Every place of employment I have had the privilege of working at, there have been numerous colleagues who have said, "I notice that you always have what you need," or will come and say, you know you have everything. I thank God that he gives me more than enough to help others. What makes you wealthy is your thinking, not your bank accounts or investments. Those things are temporary.

Prayer

Father God in the name of Jesus, I come to you on behalf of _____, *and I ask that you would open the windows of Heaven and pour out a blessing that they can't contain. Lord, your Word says that you supply the needs that we have. You even know what we need before we even ask. Lord, show yourself strong in this situation, and I will forever give you the glory. Amen*

Meditation "First of all, then, I urge that supplications, prayers, intercessions, and thanksgivings be made for all people. **1Timothy 2:1**

- 2 Chronicles 7:1-3;12
- Psalm 25:14
- Psalm 25:4-5
- Psalm 25:8-10
- Psalm 29:1-2
- Psalm 4:8
- Psalm 5:1-3
- Psalm 1:3
- Psalm 4:1
- Revelation 12:11

Prayer of Thanksgiving

Thanksgiving: "the expression of gratitude, especially to God." (Oxford Language, 8.4.20).

- Philippians 4:5
- Psalm 145:10
- Psalm 35:18
- Psalm 79:13

Prayer

Lord, I bless and praise your holy name. You are my God and my rock. You are my fortress and my very present help in the time of trouble. I exalt you for all that you do. Thank you for choosing me and for calling me your own. Thank you for your constant provision. Thank you for healing every aspect of my life and working behind the scenes on my behalf. Thank you for settling every issue. Thank you for being my hiding place. Thank you for being my battle-ax and rear guard. Thank you for your hand of protection that covers my life and my family. In Jesus' name, amen.

Prayer of Worship

Worship: the feeling or expression of reverence and adoration for a deity." (Oxford Dictionary).

Set aside a special place and time to worship the Lord. The Word of God says that we can only worship the Lord in spirit and in truth. Worship is a lifestyle. One of the things that I love about the Lord is when I wake up, he gives me a song, and that song usually carries me through the day. Once I get out of bed, I play that song. It takes me straight into the presence of God. The Holy Spirit usually takes over and reveals certain things to me or brings confirmation where it is needed. When this first started happening, I would get this warm sensation that would take over my body. I used to be afraid of it until I realized that it was the Holy Spirit of God resting upon me and in me.

Worship reveals the true nature of God through pure intimacy. It is in worship where we take on the very heart of God, brings you into this presence, and our characters are changed. The Holy Spirit speaks to us as we worship and gives us instruction. We are healed in Worship.

- One day as these men were worshiping the Lord and fasting, the Holy Spirit said, "Appoint Barnabas and Saul for the special work to which I have called them." So after more fasting and prayer, the men laid their hands on them and sent them on their way. **Acts 13:2-3**

- And they went, Jesus met them and greeted them. And they ran to him, grasped his feet, and worshiped him. **Matthew 28:9**

- For God is spirit, and those who worship him must worship him in spirit and in truth. **John 4:24**

Prayer of Consecration

Consecration: "the action of making or declaring something, typically of church, sacred." (Oxford Dictionary).

Consecrate: "to make or declare scare; to devote irrevocably to the worship of God." (Merriam-Webster dictionary).

Irrevocable: unable to change. It does not end and remains the same.

He went on a little farther and bowed with his face to the ground, praying, "My Father! If it is possible, let this cup of suffering be taken away from me. Yet I want your will to be done, not mine." (Matthew 26:39). Christ knew that his time had come and that he was about to face death. We all know that death is permanent. I am not sure if the disciples' faces flashed before Christ's face when he prayed this prayer or even if he thought about his mom, but we do know that he wanted God's will to be done more than his own.

Whenever I consecrate myself, I am seeking God and not man. These are times when I fast and set specific times to spend with him just for clarity. Consecrate yourselves by denying yourselves the very things you desire. Die to the things that keep you out of his will and entering into what God desires. Be ye holy because our Father is holy. Most people start the year off consecrating themselves by abstaining from certain foods, desires, entertainment so they can hear from God for the year. This can be done throughout the year. Start with a few hours a day until you are able to make it one day and build upon that. You will see your life and the lives of those with whom you have relationships really change. Give yourselves totally to the Lord.

Prayer:

Lord, I repent of my sins. I commit my life and my body to you and you alone. Lord, whatever doors I opened through sin that caused my body to be defiled, I ask that you reveal it and remove that which is not holy and make it Holy. I release myself from blood covenants made by my ancestors and others consecrated to idols, devil worshippers, witchcraft, sexual sin, lustful desire, and immorality. The blood of Jesus is cleansing me from it. I release myself and my seed from this defilement. We are holy because you are holy. Make the root of this family holy and burn everything that is not of you out of the linage or in my bloodline. It stops with me. In Jesus' name, amen.

Most people do not understand that their choices can defile their seeds. Many years ago, I was sitting in a church service where one of the elders said that the Lord had revealed to him that many people in the congregation were not prospering because there were people in their families who were members of certain ungodly organizations. There was an altar call after the message was delivered. I responded to the altar call because I knew that my family has connections to one of those organizations. After service, I went home, and after eating, I felt ill. I had a headache that would not stop. I decided to relax in the tub. As I rested, I fell asleep in the tub. I really don't know how long I was asleep, but I do remember the telephone ringing and my daughter coming into the bathroom and said mommy, "Ms. …. Is on the phone." When she gave me the phone, I told her that I was glad that she had called because I went to sleep in the tub and when I woke up the water had reached my nose.

When I conducted some research on that organization, it was far from godly but came in the form of a church organization. A note to the wise, before you commit to any organization, do the research. Especially focus on who created it and why. Ask God to reveal what organizations or functions your family has ties to, and asked him to break those things off you and your seed.

Prayer of Defense, Employing God's Word

- **Psalm 7:** In this chapter, David is asking God to watch over him. To protect him from those who have been accusing him. We all have fallen prey to those who desire to persecute us. In this scripture, David began to sing before the Lord, making a melody out of what he was facing. There will be times when we are faced with similar situations. Just pray. Yes, it can be challenging, and you may want to take matters into your own hands, but this doesn't allow God to move on your behalf.

  Prayer: *Father God, in the name of Jesus, I come to you seeking your hand of protection from those who are falsely accusing me, those who have brought accusations against me, and who desire to persecute me. I ask that you vindicate me and that you would restore all the damage that has been done. Father, I am looking to you for help. In Jesus' name, amen.*

- **Psalm 55**: David, the Psalmist, requests that God turn His ear to his cry for help. He is asking God to listen to him and attend to his supplication. In this passage, David is confessing that he is in need of God's intervention. He explains to God what he is feeling and what he is facing. I can remember times where I knew I was praying and knew that I needed God's help. I began to talk to the Lord. Honesty, I just prayed this scripture and kept reading it until I was assured that God would answer me. The best prayer is praying the word of God itself. Turn to this passage of scripture and read it out loud and declare it over yourself until you get results.

- **Psalm 69**: Once again, David cries out to God concerning his enemies, trials, and afflictions. David lived a life in constant battle from tending sheep, running for his life, and constant battles to protect God's children.

  Prayer: *Lord, I acknowledge that I need you. I am overwhelmed with all that I am facing. There are many things that I am faced with, and there are those who seek my ruin. I need your help. I know that you will not turn away my prayers and that you hear me from the moment I pray. Lord, I need your help. Please do not let my enemies triumph over me and disgrace me. In Jesus' name, amen.*

Praying in the Spirit

Pray in the Spirit at all times and on every occasion. Stay alert and be persistent in your prayers for all believers everywhere. ***Ephesians 6:18***

Being filled with the Holy Spirit and praying in the Spirit are totally different. Many years ago, I had a dear friend who spent a considerable amount of time praying in the spirit and taught me to do the same. To this day, I remember days where I would get calls just to check-in and to see how my day was going. On days where I received calls at work, and it was rough, they would say, since you are at work and can't pray, I'm going to pray in the spirit for you and would pray as long as I did not get an interruption. There have been times where I've done the same exact thing for others.

There are benefits to praying in the spirit. Let me be clear, praying in the spirit is not for show or to make you appear spiritually deep. That is a guaranteed miss. Praying in the spirit builds your faith, and it builds your confidence in God.

The more you pray in the Spirit, you will see healing in your body. Receive confidence to pray for others and see them as well as you delivered. Praying in the spirit will fight off the enemy and his demons. He does not have the gift of interpretation, neither can he comprehend what you and God are discussing. It also allows you to hear the voice of God with clarity. You will receive insight into things that can only be revealed by the Spirit himself. Remember that it is the Spirit that makes intercession for us and is the perfect prayer.

Some assignments will not be given or completed unless praying in the Spirit takes place. For those of you who do not believe that it takes all of this will never experience the fullness of God nor the power, he has ordained for you without it. Some things in your life are only revealed while praying in the Spirit. There have been times where I have prayed in the Spirit, and family members, friends, acquaintances have flashed before my face or fell in my spirit. As I prayed, I called out their name and continued to pray in the Spirit. Later I would hear from them or someone connected to them, and I was very grateful that I yielded to the Holy Ghost's prodding and prayed. We not only usher in God's will by praying this way, but we do damage to the enemy's kingdom and his plan.

I would encourage you to seek God in this area and if you no longer use your gift, ask God to refill you with His Spirit, and use your gift. Think about it this way; you go out of your way to purchase a gift for someone; you carefully thought of just the right gift, went to numerous stores, shopped online, and finally found it. This gift took every dime you had just to purchase it, and when you gave them the gift, they never used it. You would be so disheartened, especially because this was all they talked about and wanted. The very day you give it to them, it's received with little thought or gratitude. If you are honest, you would not want to give them anything else.

There are many resources available to help you a greater understanding of the different types and prayer and how to use them effectively for results. Ask the Holy Spirit to help you to apply them to every area of your life.

Workplace Prayer

Father God, in the name of Jesus, I come to you this morning asking you to guide me as I prepare for work. Release your angels ahead of me to watch over me as I travel today. I pray for your divine hand of protection as I go about my workday. Let love be my guide. Give me favor with every person I meet or conduct business within the marketplace. Give me the grace to work pleasingly unto you and according to your statutes and standards, instead of that men. I acknowledge that I need your help today.

Lord, Your Word says that I should pray for those who have authority over me so that it will be well with me. I forgive every person in authority who has ever disappointed or hurt me so that I can serve with a heart of gratitude and not regret. Make my way prosperous. I pray for the overall well-being of my supervisor and his or her family. Let us quickly agree for the betterment of this organization. When I do not understand the decisions implemented that affect me, give me the correct response.

I pray for this organization and its leaders. Give our leaders what they need to support the organization and its employees. Watch over, keep, and direct every employer and the employees. I cover them and their families in the blood of Jesus. Dispatch the angels you have given charge over them to protect, direct, guide, deliver and watch over them in this season.

Lord, I pray for my adversaries in the workplace. Your Word says that we should quickly agree with them and that you would vindicate your children. Please release vindication where I need it. Teach those who are in authority over me to understand who I am as a person and let them see your image in me. Guide their heart in my favor. Your Word says that the hand of the king is in your hand and that you turn it in the direction you desire. Lord, let it work out in my favor. Psalm 138:8 says that you will perfect that which concerns me; that your mercy endures forever. Lord, please do not forsake the works of your own hand. Fill this place with your love, kindness, and compassion. Fill every position with those who have a heart after you and those who have a heart to take care of others' needs.

We need people who have a strong work ethic, morals, values, and who operate in integrity. Let those whom we encounter experience the love of Christ.

Give us strength on the days we are weak. Teach us to stay humble. Remove every hindrance that will try to block our success and our progress.

When dealing with difficult situations, circumstances and people, give us a supernatural grace that only comes from you, especially on days when we're not at our best. When we are frustrated and want to give up, remind us why we are here and why you gave us this assignment. Lord, when our season is over, make our transition smooth.

Lord, I acknowledge that there are days when I struggle, and I am asking for your guidance, direction, and help. Help us to be slow to speak, slow to anger, and quick to listen and understand. Let us be faithful stewards over that which you have entrusted us. Give us a serving spirit, forgive our murmuring, and complaining. Make this company's name great. Let staffing issues be resolved quickly, timely, and handled professionally. Give us a strategic strategy for each day. Let us exceed our goals and let others take notice of us and our work ethic as an example of who we really are. Let their experience with this organization reflect you. In Jesus' name, amen.

Prayer for Health and Wholeness

Beloved, I pray that you may prosper in all things and be in health, just as your soul prospers. **3 John 1:2**

God, you desire that we are in good health and prosper as our soul prospers. My body is your temple, the place where you abide. It is your will that I am a good steward over this body. It is imperative that I nourish it well with foods that provide sustenance and provides support for growth. It is your good pleasure that no sickness or disease has a place within my body. God, you created my body and called it "good." It is the physical house that I reside in to carry out the assignment you have given me on this earth. I declare that every tissue, cell, and organ in my body will function how you intended, God. No sickness or disease can attach itself to my body. I walk in divine health. For God has redeemed us from destruction; He has satisfied us with good things so that our youth is renewed as the eagles. We shall soar high even when we are old. (Psalm 103:2-5) No sickness or disease comes nigh our dwelling. (Psalm 91) Lord, you satisfy us with long life, and I will give you praise and worship you all the days of my life. In Jesus' name, amen.

Praying For The Lost

Lord, your word says the fruit of the righteous is a tree of life, and he who wins souls is wise according to Proverbs 11:30. 1 Peter 3:9 says that the Lord is not slack concerning his promise, as some count slackness, but is longsuffering toward us, not willing that any should perish but that all should come to repentance. Lord, give me the wisdom to win those who are lost. I know that you do not want anyone to perish or die outside of you and your will. Show me those whom you have given to me as an assignment to draw to your kingdom. In Jesus' name, amen.

Who has the Lord placed on your heart, which is out of his will and in need of salvation? Commit to praying the following prayer concerning them until you get a release from God.

Lord, it is not your will that _____ perish but that _____ comes to repentance. Draw them by your Spirit since no man can come to you unless your Spirit draws them. Thank you for being long -suffering concerning _____ and thank you for their salvation. In Jesus' name, amen.

Praying To Leave An Inheritance To You Children Or Seed.

A good man leaveth an inheritance to his children's children: and the wealth of the sinner is laid up for the just. **Proverbs 13:22**

Lord, I know that you supply our needs according to your riches in glory through Christ Jesus. I know that an inheritance is more than money. Lord, teach me to leave an inheritance of love, values, principles, self-discipline, wisdom, a prayer life, and generational wealth so what I have accomplished in life will not go to waste or be used unwisely. I pray that my children (seed) would not be considered or deem wicked so that all that is accomplished would not be lost. In Jesus' name, amen.

Praying For The Restoration Of Family.

Lord, your word says that according to Proverbs 6:16-19 these six things that Lord hates, Yes, seven are an abomination to Him: a proud look, a lying tongue, hands that shed innocent blood, a heart that devises wicked plans, a false witness who speaks lies and one who sows discord among the brethren. Lord, it pleases you that family can dwell together in unity according to Psalm 133:1. Lord, I ask that you would forgive us for not honoring your Word concerning family. Forgive us for every time we have not honored what your Word has said concerning family. Family is so important to you until you created the family before other things. Give us a heart to forgive those who have hurt us and cause them to walk in forgiveness toward us for what we have done as well. Lord, restore our families so that the truth of your Word would be evident in our lives and that we will complete the assignment that you have given us in the area of ministry concerning family. Tear down generational stubbornness that causes unforgiveness that was passed from one generation to the next. Heal us and remove every hindrance that would try to stop our progress in this area. Jesus' name, amen.

Prayer When Facing the Enemy

Read Psalm 35:1-28

The Lord reminded me one day of a passage in scripture that he had given me in the past, and I began to use it in my prayers for a current situation. I saw one of my accusers exit the building on the day my resignation was to end, and the next one left within thirty days of me praying Psalm 35. At one point in my career, I was faced with so much opposition until I did not know what to do. I was on the verge of giving up. I called several people that I know and requested prayer. Rather than respond to the evil I was facing, I let the building and found myself walking down the street praying in the spirit and talking to the Lord. At the end of my walk, I noticed that I was standing in front of a church and a restaurant. I asked God to send me help, and I surrendered to Him. My prayer for years has been that I would be an effective witness of the Lord to those I encounter.

I was at a breaking point, and I knew I was not in a place where God had released me to walk away as I have done in times past. The Lord allowed me to get myself together and return to work. One of the pastors from my church received a message from her secretary to pray for me and why. She called me and covered me in prayer. She also reminded me of the authority that God had given me through Jesus Christ, and we took authority over the spirit that had been harassing me for quite some time. As I returned to my desk, there was a knock at the door. A young woman stood there with a bouquet of flowers in her hands and said, "Thank you so much for helping my mom and me." A second knock on the door was another token of love. Someone witnessed what happened to me, and they reported it. God will protect you and fight your battles.

There will be days when you are tested and opposed for no apparent reason at all. Let God's Word do the work. God not only released me from that company, but he dismissed my accusers as well. On my last day of working, the director came to me and apologized for everything that I had to endure while working there. It takes a big person to come to you and apologize for anything.

I am sharing this testimony because some of you may be in this situation and feel like giving up. One of my dearest friends reminds me all that time that only God controls the assignment. I believe that he controls both the assignment and what happens while you are on it as well. You may never receive an apology, but God will deal with every situation we face in his way and in his time. Understand that God is an enemy to your enemy and a friend to your friends.

I am truly grateful for all of my friends who take the time to pray for me constantly. I charge each of you today to cover your friends and families in prayer continuously. You may never know the difference you made in their day, especially in their workplace. Another dear friend gave me a birthday gift one day and instructed me to take what was in this bag to the workplace. She said, place this on your desk as a reminder to put on the Full Armor of God and let this shield remind you of the weapons you have in prayer.

A Prayer Of Strengthening Against The Wicked

On days where you know you are facing evil, read Psalm 37 out loud and meditate on it. It will serve as a reminder that if we do what God commands us, he will avenge us. Psalm 37 covers all types of adversities and obstacles we face. It addresses how wicked people lie in wait for an opportunity to slay or destroy you. There are times in the book of Psalms where David is praying for God to destroy his enemies, and in other parts, he reminds himself that the godly will prevail no matter what. Let's learn to take his approach. Take some time to review this passage and highlight or write out what is speaking to you in this present moment. What is God showing you? Can you apply any of this to your current situation?

Getting Dressed For Prayer

Father God, I put on the full armor of God this morning as according to your Word. I put on the helmet of salvation that is mine because of the shed blood of Jesus

Christ. I cover my mind in the blood of Jesus. Let this mind be in you as it is in Christ Jesus. Lord, you will keep my mind in peace if it stays on you.

I put on the breastplate of righteousness. Righteousness comes from Christ, Jesus alone. I guard my heart with all diligence. Keep my heart from being evil. Give me a heart of flesh and remove the stony parts that separate me from the truth of your Word and the truth of who you really are in my life.

I put on the buckle of truth this morning by putting on the truth of your Word. Keep me from lies, the deceptiveness of man, and the errors of this world that would cause me to think in a way that contradicts who I am in you. I block lies told from others about who I am and what I haven't done—deception of what you have said about me. Keep me from being deceived by others and from being a deceiver.

I put on the shoes of peace this morning. Peace that comes from you and you alone. Peace of the gospel of Jesus Christ. Peace that leads to love and salvation. Man cannot comprehend the peace that comes from Jesus.

I take the sword of the spirit with the Word of God, and I cancel every assignment of the evil one who would try to attack my character, my family, and the body of Christ and our seed. I send the Word of God ahead of us this morning to set captives free and to do warfare on our behalf in the mighty name of Jesus. Lord be it according to me as it is according to your Word. In Jesus' name, amen.

PRAYER SCRIPTURES FOR SPECIFIC NEEDS

When You Are Facing Adversity

- Proverbs 3:6-8
- Psalm 1:1-13
- Psalm 14
- Psalm 15

- Psalm 30:2
- Psalm 6:8-10
- Psalm 103:3-5

When You Need the Security and Comfort That Only Comes From God

- Ecclesiastes 7:8
- Jeremiah 23:20
- Psalm 138:8
- Psalm 145:14-16

- Psalm 145:8-9
- Psalm 16
- Psalm 28:6-9
- Psalm 32
- Psalm 51:10

Godly Desires
- James 4:8
- Psalm 145:17-18
- Psalm 37:4

Drawing Near to God
- Jeremiah 29:13
- Jeremiah 33:3
- Psalm 145:18

In Need of Healing
- Exodus 15:26
- Exodus 23:25
- Isaiah 30:26
- Matthew 4:23-24

In Times of Restoration
- 2 Chronicles 7:14-16
- Joel 2:25-32
- Psalm 23:1-4

When Facing Temptation

- 1 Corinthians 10:13
- 1 Corinthians 6:12
- 1 Corinthians 9:27
- 2 Peter 2:9
- Galatians 5:1

- James 1:2-8
- Matthew 6:13
- Psalm 33:10-22
- Romans 6:18-23

My Daily Prayer Confessions

I pray this over my family, friends, and love ones consistently. As you pray for others, say their name or names where you see "I" or "me". For example, instead of "I," will rejoice and be glad in it, change to the individual's or individuals' name you are interceding for. We're commanding our day and confessing what we are expecting God to do for us. God's Word tells us that life and death are in the power of our tongue. We must confess life according to God's will and death to anything that hinders or blocks it. God's Word will not return to Him void but will accomplish what it is set out to do. Angels are dispatched to do your bidding through prayer and by the command of His Word.

*Thou shalt also decree a thing, and it shall be established unto thee: **Job 22:28***

1. This is the day the Lord has made, and in it, I shall rejoice and be glad.

2. No weapon formed against me shall prosper, and every tongue that rises itself against me, God shall condemn.

3. The Lord gives his angels charge over my life to guard and protect me from all evil.

4. The Lord daily loads my family and me with benefits. Lord, thank you for the benefit of health, healing, prosperity, deliverance, knowing your voice, clarity of vision, for directing my family and me, and for the purpose by which you have created us.

5. I decree and declare that my family and I are the head and not the tail. We are above and not beneath.

6. Every generational curse and every word curse has been broken off of our lives, and we walk in generational blessing for thousands of generations.

7. The blessing of Abraham, Isaac, and Jacob belong to us because we are the seed of Abraham.

8. The spirit of guilt, condemnation, and shame are broken off our lives.

9. Nothing by any means shall harm us as according to your Word.

10. It was for freedom that Christ has made us free. We will not be entangled in a yoke of bondage again.

11. The Lord shall increase me more and more. He will increase my children.

12. We grow in wisdom and stature and have favor with both God and man.

13. The blood of Jesus is cleansing us from everything that is not of him, which will keep us from God.

14. I cover our minds, spirit, body, and soul with the blood of Jesus. Nothing by any means shall harm us.

15. Create a clean heart in us, renew in us a right spirit, and do not take your Holy Spirit from us.

16. Forgive us from all of our sins, past failures, and for the times that we have not lived according to your Word or purpose.

17. Remove everything from us that is contrary to your word and what you haven't spoken over us.

18. I cancel every lying, deceptive, and manipulative spirit that would try to operate against us individually or collectively.

19. When we feel like giving up, remind us that you are at work in us and that you will be faithful to complete that which you have started in us.

20. Lord, keep us from evil people; keep evil people from us, but most of all, keep us from being evil.

In conclusion, I pray that you get the results that you are seeking. God will answer your prayers. Just keep pressing towards and confessing what you want to see manifest. It will take some time but do not give up in the process. On days when you do not feel like praying, ask God to grace you. In my prayer closet, I have the names of my family, friends, those who are close to me, and any prayer request that I receive written on a large poster to ensure that I cover them in prayer. There are days when I only pray for a select few, and there are days when I cover all of them. I used this along with scripture as a foundation. There are times when the Holy Spirit guides me differently. I am saying this to say start somewhere!

Meditation

- Psalms 121:1-8
- Psalms 127:1-5
- Psalms 128
- Psalms 133
- Psalms 136
- Psalms 138:7-8
- Psalms 139:13-18

CHAPTER KEYS

1. Remember to dress for the battle.
2. Reflecting on scripture will help you build a foundation in prayer and the word of God.
3. Praying the word of God gets results.
4. God has a plan for both the godly and the wicked.

Prophetic Declarations Over Your Life

You shall raise up a new generation of intercessors from your own lineage. No matter what it looks like, God will sustain you and turn everything around in your favor. May the Lord take sickness and lack from among you. May he heal your land, water, bread, and take every illness from your life. May he continue to sustain you in every area of your life. May he heal you from past hurts and wounds. May he heal you from those who hurt you and never asked for forgiveness. May he comfort you where you need it the most. The Lord will break every generational curse off of you and your seed, and you will walk in generational blessings and favor that come from God. You will walk uprightly, and the Lord will bless a thousand generations because of your righteousness. Walk in the favor of God and be blessed in every way, in every area of your lives. In Jesus' name, amen!

IN CLOSING

When my children were growing up, if they asked me if they could do something, my response would be, "It is fine with me but ask your dad." Over time, I noticed they would come and go, do whatever they were doing, and I had no idea. Whenever I asked them, "Where are you going?" or "Who said you could do this or that?" their response became, "I asked my dad." Interestingly, I would say, "Nobody asked me, and remember you have two parents." One by one, they all responded, "Whenever we ask you something, your response is to ask your dad, so we just asked our dad." Honestly, I remembered feeling jealous over this feeling as if I didn't have any say. My husband said that I taught them this, and they just did what was taught to them. One day the Holy Spirit of God said to me, "What if you took everything straight to your dad just like your kids do?" Yes, take everything to your dad. What do you think would happen? I began to think of how much different life could be if I just took it straight to my dad. I learned from this that we spend too much time asking others for their opinion and what they think. When all we have to do is ask *our* dad. We do not need the middleman, just go straight to the source of the one who has the answers, and he will send confirmation of what should be done.

As we go about our day, there are times when we have moments of uncertainty, discomfort, grief, fear of the unknown, and need to be strengthened. On those days, meditate on the Word of God, receive comfort and strength through his word. God is near to those who call upon him, and he is a very present help in the time of trouble. The world we live in needs God and prayer like never before. In the book of Psalms, David asked himself, "Soul, why are you so downcast?" Life has a way of signing you up for things you never wanted or enlisted in. God has a way of using those things to bring you closer to him while giving you the spiritual strength you need to survive. God has commanded us in his word to meditate on it day and night. David hid the Word of God in his heart that he might not sin against God.

While eating breakfast one morning with the kids, one of them asked, "How do you know when God is speaking to you?" As I began to explain my *mommy's* version of how to know when God is speaking to you, one of my sons said, "It's not that God is not speaking. You're just not listening. You have to be in a position to hear." He later said this to me, and I never forgot it. "Mom, a warrior's greatest weapons are time and patience." Now I speak this to you; your greatest weapons are time, patience, and perseverance.

Keep a notepad and writing utensil near your bed and in your prayer room. Use them to record your dreams, prayer requests, or assignments. Record what the Lord shares with you during your quiet time, either by his voice or by his written word. Whenever someone asks you to pray for them, take a moment to stop and pray right then. This will ensure that your prayer matches the request and that both of you are touching and agreeing on the same thing. Not all prayer assignments should be discussed with others or prayed with others. Understand that certain assignments are for you alone. When you have been entrusted with a person's prayer request, do not disclose your assignment to others. This will violate the person who made the request. Get permission if you need to agree with anyone other than the person you are praying for. This will ensure that the person does not feel betrayed or exposed.

Share your testimony when led. You never know who needs encouragement. Be led by the Holy Spirit in this area. Remember, Joseph and his dream. In a prophetic dream, God showed Joseph what would become of his family. Due to a lack of maturity, his family did not understand the full magnitude of God's plan for their lives. His eagerness to share led him to be betrayed by the ones who should have protected him. You may not see all of your prayers answered on this side but remember that God will honor any promise or covenant he made with you. Remember Abraham, Rachel, David, and your ancestor who believed for better. Never give up on your prayers, dreams, or God's promises. Remember that it's not our will but God's will. We learned this principle from Jesus when he was in the garden, praying about what was to come. In conclusion, here is my prayer for you, the CHOSEN INTERCESSOR,

Heavenly Father, I come to you in the name of Jesus, thanking you in advance for every person's life who will read this book. I pray that you meet the needs of your people, both naturally and spiritually. Teach them to pray not just for themselves but for the needs of your people. Teach them to pray according to your will. Invade their space with your presence and fill them again and again with your precious

Holy Spirit. In Jesus' name, may their days be filled with purpose, and may you continue to make their ways prosperous.

Lord, I pray that their joy is complete. God grant them the desires of their hearts. May you hear from heaven and answer their prayers quickly. May the dew of the morning be a refresher and a sign to them of your faithfulness and rest upon every heart.

Lord, send help from your holy sanctuary and fill them with a renewed strength daily. May each of them experience rest from all of their troubles.

My personal prayer for you, the reader, is that your days be filled with joy, peace, love, and a sense of newness. May you experience God's grace, healing, and freedom. May you receive all that God has in store for you. May you walk in total restoration, deliverance, and the abundance that Christ exchanged for you through his works on the cross. Peace to you from God the Father. May the blessing of the Lord overtake you in this season. May his blessings make you rich and add no sorrow to you.

Father, forgive us in the name of Jesus for anything that we have done that is not pleasing to you. Forgive those who have trespassed against us, whether intentionally or not. Lead us not into temptation but deliver us from all manner of evil. Lord, thank you for being our Father, Protector, Healer, Provider, and our Deliver. Lord, I ask that you give them wisdom, knowledge, and discernment over every decision they have to make. I block every evil, deceptive, lying, manipulative spirit that is at work in any area of their lives or their families' lives, through doors that were unknowingly opened through their bloodline, especially from any manner of evil that is at work through time released assignments of bloodshed covenants made with the adversary.

You will deliver your children from the hand of the evil one, from the hands of men, and nothing by any means shall harm them as according to your word. I declare it done according to your word, will, and your way. Experience God's peace, victory, healing, grace, and freedom today! In the powerful name of Jesus, AMEN!

APPENDIX

GOD TRACKS

DATE:_____

What am I facing today? _____

_____

_____

What does scripture say about this situation/circumstance? Use scripture as a foundation to build your prayer request. _____

_____

_____

Prayer Request_____

_____

_____

Foundational Scriptures_____

_____

_____

Prayer of Gratitude and Thanks_____

_____

_____

What am I thankful for?_____

_____

_____

Praise Moment_____

_____

_____

Ask yourself, did I pray for someone else or their circumstances?

_____

_____

_____

PRAYER ANSWERED DATE: _____

DATE:_____

What am I facing today? _____

_____

_____

What does scripture say about this situation/circumstance? Use scripture as a foundation to build your prayer request. _____

_____

_____

Prayer Request_____

_____

_____

Foundational Scriptures_____

_____

_____

Prayer of Gratitude and Thanks_____

_____

_____

What am I thankful for?_____

_____

_____

Praise Moment_____

_____

_____

Ask yourself, did I pray for someone else or their circumstances?

_____

_____

_____

PRAYER ANSWERED DATE: _____

DATE:_____

What am I facing today? _____

_____

_____

What does scripture say about this situation/circumstance? Use scripture as a foundation to build your prayer request. _____

_____

_____

Prayer Request_____

_____

_____

Foundational Scriptures_____

_____

_____

Prayer of Gratitude and Thanks_____

_____

_____

What am I thankful for?_____

_____

_____

Praise Moment_____

_____

_____

Ask yourself, did I pray for someone else or their circumstances?

_____

_____

_____

PRAYER ANSWERED DATE: _____

DATE:_____

What am I facing today? _____

_____

_____

What does scripture say about this situation/circumstance? Use scripture as a foundation to build your prayer request. _____

_____

_____

Prayer Request_____

_____

_____

Foundational Scriptures_____

_____

_____

Prayer of Gratitude and Thanks_____

_____

_____

What am I thankful for?_____

_____

_____

Praise Moment_____

_____

_____

Ask yourself, did I pray for someone else or their circumstances?

_____

_____

_____

PRAYER ANSWERED DATE: _____

DATE:_____

What am I facing today? _____

_____

_____

What does scripture say about this situation/circumstance? Use scripture as a foundation to build your prayer request. _____

_____

_____

Prayer Request_____

_____

_____

Foundational Scriptures_____

_____

_____

Prayer of Gratitude and Thanks_____

_____

_____

What am I thankful for?_____

_____

_____

Praise Moment_____

_____

_____

Ask yourself, did I pray for someone else or their circumstances?

_____

_____

_____

PRAYER ANSWERED DATE: _____

ABOUT THE AUTHOR

Erica Bethely is a graduate of Hinds Community College and Kennesaw State University. She currently resides in Georgia with her spouse and their children.

Erica is a teacher of the Word of God. She is the founder and leader of a dynamic Women's Bible Study and prayer group. She is known for encouraging others. Erica has a passion for winning people to Christ, for those who have lost hope and desire restoration in any area of their lives. Her greatest desire is to raise intercessors for the Kingdom of God. She firmly believes in the Word of God and the Power of Prayer. Both have made a lasting impact on both her and her family.

Erica's advocacy is for the elderly and disabled while making a lasting impact on families through ministry. We are more than conquers. We are chosen intercessors, equipped for every good work in us through Christ Jesus. Erica believes that she was BORN TO PRAY.....

Made in the USA
Coppell, TX
22 December 2020